CONTENTS

KU-446-576

TO THE READER

Most people find criminals interesting. Our newspapers are full of their stories, and there is no shortage of crime fiction in books, television programmes and films. Most criminals, however, are far from being romantic villains. Some of them are to be feared, but most of them you would pity, as you might someone who is ill. Crime, in fact, is very like a disease in our society.

To deal with our criminals we have our police forces and our prisons. This book will tell you how these important services developed from the late eighteenth century down to the middle years of the nineteenth century. You will see that they made progress then, and they have made even more down to the present day. But our criminals are still with us and are still as active as ever. Why should this be?

This book will tell you a little of what was done in the past. When you have read it, you might well think about what should be done in the future.

PART ONE
POLICE AND PRISONS BEFORE REFORM

1 Prisons in the late Eighteenth Century

One day, nearly two hundred years ago, an Englishman was travelling in a coach through Prussia, in northern Germany. The road was bad, and in places was so narrow that two vehicles could not pass. The rule was that on approaching a narrow section a coachman should sound his horn to warn traffic coming the other way. This the Englishman's driver was careful to do and he was rather surprised to find his way blocked by a coach that had given no warning. The owner was a messenger of the King of Prussia who thought himself too important a man to bother with the rules of the road. Of course, he expected the Englishman to order his coachman to back out of the way. The Englishman quietly refused. His coachman had sounded his horn, as the law required; the royal Messenger's had not. The argument went on for a long time. The messenger grew angry and made threats about what could happen to foreigners who dared to interrupt the King's business, but the Englishman remained calm and determined. In the end it was the messenger's coach that had to back.

The Englishman's name was John Howard. He always behaved in that same quiet determined way. Once he had set his mind on doing something, then nothing could turn him from it. Most of his time and energy he spent in working for prison reform.

Howard first became interested in prisons when he was made Sheriff of Bedfordshire in 1773. He was horrified at what he found. He wrote, 'Looking into the prisons I beheld scenes of calamity which I grew daily more and more anxious to

*alleviate.** I beheld in many of them a complication of distress.'
He decided to give the rest of his life to the reform of the
prisons since, as he said, 'I could not enjoy my ease and
leisure in the neglect of an opportunity offered me by Provi-
dence of attempting the relief of the miserable'.

Gaolers tried to obstruct him and trick him, but he grew
wise to their methods. He would not leave a prison until he
had visited every part of it. Nor was it enough for him to see.
He had a little pair of scales to weigh the rations and he had a
tape with which he measured everything—the height, width
and breadth of the cells and wards, the size of the windows
and doors, the area of the courtyards, the height of the walls.
All this he noted and wrote down in a simple, unemotional
language that let the facts speak for themselves.

In 1777 he produced his 'State of the Prisons', and continued making his reports until he died in 1790. From then
onwards prison reform might move slowly; at times it might
even be neglected. It was, however, quite impossible to forget
how much it was needed.

We will now see what Howard found in the prisons of those
times.

THE PRISONERS

Today we think of a prison as a place where we send men or
women who have done wrong. They are there as a punishment
and, we hope, to be reformed. The common gaol in the eighteenth century was not used for such purposes. Certainly no
one was ever reformed in it—quite the reverse, as we shall see.
Nor was it intended as a place of punishment, even though
every sort of cruelty was found inside its walls. Most of the
people in gaol were not criminals at all: they were debtors. In
the eighteenth century a *creditor* could have a person who
owed him money imprisoned until the debt was paid.

Another group of people in gaol would be those arrested for

* Words printed like this are explained in the Glossary on p. 104.

2

an offence, but waiting for their trial. Although in law they were still innocent, they might find themselves waiting a long time. Trials were infrequent. They might take place every six months, they might take place every year. In some towns they were every three years, and in Hull they were every seven years.

Finally we come to those who really were criminals. Some of these were indeed serving a sentence of imprisonment ordered by a court, but many of the *felons* would be waiting for a punishment of some other kind— *transportation*, the *hulks*, or, at worst, a hanging.

PRISON ADMINISTRATION

The people responsible for the prisons were the visiting magistrates, who were supposed to inspect the place and see that all was well. This was a most unpleasant job, and, because of the infectious diseases common in prisons, it was also dangerous. Very few magistrates were like Howard, so that prisons sometimes went without inspection for several years.

Consequently the way the prison was managed depended

Bambridge on Trial

almost entirely on the gaoler. Unfortunately gaolers were not normally men of good character and as they had no salaries, their only concern was to make as much money as possible out of their prisoners. On p. 3 you can see a notorious gaoler, Bambridge, on trial for murdering some of his prisoners. His instruments of torture are being used as evidence.

Each gaol had its own scale of fees that the keeper was allowed to charge. For example, some of those at Newgate were as follows:

Keeper's Entrance Fee   3*s*.
Keeper's Discharge Fee 6*s*. 1o*d*.
Turnkeys   2*s*.

The gaoler also charged for such things as putting on irons, or taking them off. Here you can see a picture of a prisoner in irons.

It could easily happen that the fees would come to more than a fine. For example, Howard found two sailors who had been fined a shilling each, owed fees of over a pound. They had been in prison for some time, since they could not find the money, and the gaoler would not let them go until they paid.

Prisoner in Irons

Indeed, fees had to be paid even by people found innocent by the courts. It was the sight of such folk being dragged back to prison that first started Howard on his investigations.

The gaoler did not content himself with fees. For him the inmates of the prison were so many captive customers. He could supply them with food, firing, bedding, furniture and games. For example we find these charges from Newgate:

Prisoners—two in a bed   1*s*. 3*d*. per week
Prisoners—one in a bed   2*s*. 6*d*. per week

Probably the largest source of profit was the *tap-room*. Here prisoners who could afford it bought drink of all kinds. Not surprisingly, the tap-room was often a centre of disturbance.

Prisoners who could afford none of these extra luxuries were left in filth and misery, living on what they could obtain from charity.

BUILDINGS

In the eighteenth century there was no set plan for prisons. Each was different, though in the larger ones you could expect to find the same type of accommodation.

In the first place there was a section of the prison for debtors. This was divided into two, the 'masters' side' and the 'common side'. The masters' side was for those who could afford to pay for those comforts that the prison had to offer. A man might be able to afford a separate room for himself, or even a whole suite of rooms. Others might share a room with one or two fellow prisoners of their own choice. The 'common side' was for debtors who could afford to pay little or nothing. Usually they were herded together in one room.

Between the two there was a courtyard where the prisoners could walk or play games during the day.

Another section of the prison was for criminals—the 'felons ward' as it was called. The felons were herded together in one room, like the common side debtors. They, too, had a court-yard they could use in the daytime.

It was not always the practice to have separate prisons for men and women, but Newgate did provide separate wards for them.

That the buildings were grim goes without saying. Howard describes the condemned cells at Newgate. They were nine feet high, nine feet long, and six feet wide. The upper part of the cell had a narrow window, three feet by one foot. The doors were four inches thick. The walls were lined with planks, studded with nails. He adds:

> 'I was told by those who attended them that criminals who had affected an air of boldness during their trial, and appeared quite unconcerned at the pronouncing of sentence upon them, were struck with horror, and shed tears when brought to these darksome solitary abodes.'

Floors were often damp. To make things worse, there might be no beds, possibly even no straw. If they did have straw, then it might not be changed nearly often enough.

Howard said:

> 'If by any means they get a little, it is not changed for months together, so that it is offensive and almost worn to dust. Some lie upon rags, others upon bare floors.'

Heating was unheard of, for there were no chimneys, and no allowance for coal.

FOOD

Those who could afford to pay had whatever food they wanted. Those who had no money were in considerable distress.

An old Act of Parliament, passed in 1572, allowed Justices of the Peace to raise a small rate in order to buy bread for poor prisoners. This allowance was known as the 'county bread'. Unfortunately, there were many things wrong with this system.

The allowance was usually twopence a day, but in the eighteenth century twopence bought only half the bread that it did in the sixteenth. Moreover, the price of wheat varied considerably from year to year, depending on the harvest. Again, gaolers were not above making a profit out of the miserable allowance, so that prisoners got less to eat than they were entitled to. It might be not more than half a pound a day, so that a man could easily eat a two-day ration for breakfast, and then he would have to fast for forty-eight hours. Howard said:

'Such of them as at their *commitment* were in health, came out almost famished, scarce able to move, and for weeks incapable of any labour.'

Finally, the county allowance was only for convicted felons. Prisoners waiting trial, and possibly innocent, had none: prisoners who had served their sentence, but could not pay the fees for their release, also went without. Debtors, too, were excluded. Howard pointed out that while the county gave bread to highwaymen, housebreakers and murderers, it gave nothing to debtors, who had been guilty of no crime at all; all that these unfortunate people could rely on was charity.

'I have often seen these prisoners eating their water-soup (bread boiled in mere water) and heard them say: "We are locked up and almost starved to death!" '

PRISON SANITATION AND HEALTH

These are the conditions Howard found in Newgate:

'In three or four rooms there were near 150 women crowded together, many young creatures with the old and hardened, some of whom had been confined upwards of two years: on the men's side, likewise there were many boys of twelve or fourteen years of age; some almost naked. In the men's *infirmary* there were only seven iron bedsteads, and there being twenty sick, some of them, naked with sores, in a miserable condition, lay on the floor with only a rag. Sewers offensive: prison not whitewashed.'

The prison was almost always dirty. There was no serious attempt at all to keep it clean. Obviously, where several people were locked up for days together, cells were bound to be filthy. A newspaper of the time said:

'The felons in this country lie worse than dogs or swine, and are kept much more uncleanly than those animals are in kennels or sties. The stench and nastiness are so *nauseous* that no person enters without the risk of his health and life.'

The gaoler was of course, mainly responsible for allowing this filth, but prisoners did little to help. Some kept dogs and fowls in their rooms. Ventilation was poor. Fresh air is free, but windows were taxed, and if there were openings there was the danger of a prisoner escaping.

The bad air clung to the walls so that it would have taken years to make those cells fit to live in, even had the gaoler been willing to make an effort. Even the clothes of a visitor became foul. Howard wrote:

'Air which has been breathed is made poisonous to a more intense degree, by the *effluvia* from the sick, and what else in prisons is offensive. My reader will judge of its malignity when I assure him that my clothes were so offensive that in a post-chaise I could not bear the windows drawn up; and was therefore obliged to travel commonly on horseback. The leaves of my memorandum book were often so tainted, that I could not use it till after spreading it an hour or two before the fire. I did not wonder that in those journeys many gaolers made excuses and did not go with me into the felons' wards.'

Obviously, in these conditions there was bound to be disease. It was estimated that each year about one quarter of the people in prison died. While every kind of disease was found, many of them highly contagious, the most dreaded were smallpox and gaol fever. Gaol fever we know as typhus, a dangerous and very infectious disease.

Of course, gaol fever was no respecter of persons. The disease could spread from the prisoners in the dock to infect the judge and jury. Discharged prisoners carried it home to their families. Transported felons carried it to the colonies. Prisoners enlisted in the army and navy carried it into the services. In 1783 a regiment of 700 men set sail for the West Indies, but they included some criminals recruited in prison. By the time the ships reached their destination, only 70 men remained alive.

A FAVOURED PRISONER: LORD GEORGE GORDON

As you have already seen, prisoners who could afford to pay, could have many comforts. One of the most fortunate inmates of Newgate gaol was Lord George Gordon. He was there for the part he played in starting the Gordon Riots. (There is a little about these on p. 10). As Lord George was a nobleman he had rather special treatment.

Each morning he rose at eight. Two serving maids arrived and prepared his breakfast. During this meal he read his newspapers. At twelve o'clock his visitors arrived, and at two o'clock they all sat down to dinner. Usually there were about eight or ten for this meal. They ate soup, followed by fish or meat, and then a pudding. To drink, they had beer and wine. The visitors remained until 6 o'clock when they and the two maids had to leave. Lord George then had his tea, and smoked his pipe until eight in the evening, at which time he went to bed.

Sometimes there were parties. The Duke of York lent his band, and sometimes even came himself. There was music, dancing and singing. Lord George thoroughly enjoyed himself and so did his guests, save when their host insisted on entertaining them with his own favourite musical instrument— the bagpipes.

There was, however, one thing that hung like a shadow over every prisoner, rich or poor, and that was gaol fever. It was this disease which ended Lord George Gordon's imprisonment in Newgate.

Newgate had an evil reputation, and everyone in London hated the place. During the Gordon Riots of 1780 the mob had complete control of London, and they took advantage of this to destroy the prison. Here are two accounts of what happened. The first was written by the poet, George Crabbe, and the second by Lady Anne Erskine.

'I never saw anything so dreadful. The prison was a remarkably strong building, but determined to force it, they broke the gates with *crows* and climbed up the outside of the cell part; they broke the roof, tore away the rafters, and having got ladders they descended. Not *Orpheus* himself had more courage or better luck; flames all around them, and a body of soldiers expected. They defied all opposition.'

'Such a scene I never beheld, and I pray never may again. We were surrounded by flames! Six different fires with that of Newgate among the rest, towering to the clouds—being full in our view at once, and every hour in expectation of this house and beautiful chapel making a seventh. The flames all around had got to such a height that the sky was like blood, with the reflection of them. The mob so near we heard them knocking the irons off the prisoners; which, together with the shouts of those they had released, the huzzas of the rioters, and the universal confusion of the whole neighbourhood make it beyond description.'

Later, of course, order was restored and the prison was rebuilt. Unfortunately, there was no attempt to make a better building. The new prison had all the faults of the old one, as you have seen from Howard's description of it.

2 Crime and the Criminal Law

During the eighteenth century the wealth of England increased, and the towns grew in size, particularly London. One
result was that more and more people found they could make
a living from crime. In the face of this, Parliament could think
of only one remedy, and that was to make punishments severe,
in the hope of frightening criminals into good behaviour. An
increasing number of offences became punishable by death,
until, in the early nineteenth century there were as many as
two hundred capital crimes, that is, crimes for which the
punishment was death.

Here you see a picture of a public hanging about to take
place. The *ordinary* is talking to the condemned man, who is
standing in the cart with the coffin behind him.

An Execution at Tyburn

Capital crimes included, of course, murder, high treason,
riot and rebellion, but many others were quite absurd. You

could be hanged for cutting down trees, destroying *turnpikes*, bridges or locks, sending threatening letters, cutting hop-binds or breaking down the head of a fish pond so that the fish were lost. It was also a hanging matter if you stole goods worth more than 40*s*.

The severe laws did not, however, keep people from crime. So ineffective were they that at any public hanging, pick-pockets were usually at work among the crowd. This 'Punch' cartoon of 1845 shows that people thought a hanging was a spectacle—much as we would a football match.

MORAL INFLUENCE OF EXECUTIONS.

Where ave we bin? Why, to see the Cove ung, to be sure!

One reason why the death penalty did not deter, was that a criminal who committed a capital offence was most unlikely to be hung. In the first place it was very unlikely that he would be caught. Without any proper police, his chances of escape were excellent, and the majority of crimes went unde-tected. Even if the criminal was caught, he was still a long way from the gallows. He might not even be brought to trial. There was no Director of Public Prosecutions. Instead, prosecution was the duty of individual citizens and it was up to the injured party to bring charges, if he wanted justice done. Prosecution could cost a lot of time and money, and often it was just not worth the bother. Sometimes a prosecutor would not make a charge, because he had no wish to see someone hanged for a trifling offence; sometimes friends of the criminal would threaten the prosecutor and scare him off.

Even if the prosecutor was determined to go ahead, the criminal still had a good chance of an acquittal. Again, if the criminal had friends they could be useful. They could bribe or frighten witnesses, or they could commit *perjury*, swearing their companion an alibi. Bearing the death penalty in mind, the courts would usually give the accused the benefit of the doubt. However, let us again assume the worst, and say that our criminal is found guilty. It is still not likely that he will be condemned to death. The judge and jury would do their best to reduce the offence to one that was not capital. Juries were known to swear that goods of considerable value were worth only thirty-nine shillings—even a purse containing £10.

Finally, even if the judge did pass the death sentence, the criminal was still unlikely to be hanged. Four out of every five condemned to death had their sentences reduced to transportation.

In the year 1793 over 1,000 people were tried at the Old Bailey. This is what happened to them:

Acquitted	567
Transported	169
Imprisoned	129
Whipped and imprisoned	48
Made to join Army or Navy	38
Pardoned	21
Sentenced to death	68

Remember that of the sixty-eight condemned to die, only thirteen or fourteen would have been hanged. Remember, too, that the list only tells us of people brought to trial. It says nothing of the large numbers caught, but not prosecuted, and the even greater numbers never even caught.

AN EIGHTEENTH CENTURY CRIMINAL

In the eighteenth century, as now, most criminals were poor, unhappy creatures. In those days most of them could neither read nor write, so that we can discover little enough about them as individuals. Occasionally, however, there were well-educated criminals, and a few of these wrote the stories of their own lives. Such a one was James Hardy Vaux.

Vaux was born in Surrey in 1782. His father and mother led an unhappy life, so he was adopted by his grandfather, who was a solicitor. The grandfather gave him a comfortable home, and a good education, so that Vaux learnt to talk, dress and behave like a gentleman. He found this very useful when he eventually turned to crime.

At fourteen Vaux became an apprentice to a linen draper. One of his duties was to deliver goods and collect money for them, and it was this which put temptation in his way. One day he was returning to the shop, after making a delivery, when he came upon a cock-pit, that is, a place where game-cocks were made to fight each other for sport. He could not resist going inside and placing a large bet. At first all seemed to go well. The cock which Vaux had backed stretched his opponent in the dust and was just raising his head to crow in triumph. Suddenly the other bird leapt at his rival in a last burst of strength and slashed his throat.

Vaux was besieged by men who demanded their winnings, and the only thing he could do was to pay them with his employer's money. When he returned to the shop, he concealed his theft, booking the goods to the lady who had paid him. This meant of course, that the unfortunate woman would eventually have another bill, instead of her receipt.

It all seemed too easy. Vaux tried the same trick again, with success, and he also began to steal goods from the shop. He went too far, however, when he made out some bills to various customers, collected the money from them and kept it for himself. He was arrested and after seven weeks in prison was brought to trial for obtaining money by false pretences. Good luck was on his side, for he was acquitted on a point of law.

Vaux's career in crime now began in real earnest. During his stay in prison he had met a young man named Bromley. Bromley was an expert pickpocket, and before very long he had taught Vaux to become an expert as well. The two youths did not stop at picking pockets. They carried out smash and grab raids, they snatched goods from errand boys, they flung snuff in shop-keepers' eyes and robbed their tills, and they passed counterfeit coins.

For some time they made a good living for themselves, but then came disaster. They stole a handkerchief from someone's pocket and were caught in the act. The charge was stealing a handkerchief worth two shillings, and since stealing anything over one shilling 'from the person' was a capital crime, Vaux and Bromley might have been hanged. However, the jury took pity on them, and found that the handkerchief was worth only elevenpence. Vaux was sentenced to be transported for seven years.

When he arrived in New South Wales he was lucky. Thanks to his education he spent most of his time doing clerical work. Nor did he have to pay his passage back to England as was usual: he travelled as clerk to a governor who was coming home to retire.

Vaux determined to lead an honest life. However, he found that working for a living was tedious. He earned a guinea a week reading *proofs*, but this was boring and unprofitable, so he gave it up. Soon his funds ran out, and he had only a few shillings left. In despair he stole a packet that had been stowed away in a coach. To his joy it contained £50, and his money troubles were now over; but having once more taken to crime he could not give it up.

Bromley, too, had finished his seven-year sentence, and the two once more worked together. Vaux was now the master. He could act the part of a gentleman, and Bromley could not. He took the goods which Vaux stole and hid them, but normally he had to keep his distance. Vaux would not speak to him, or even look at him in public through fear of attracting suspicion.

During the day, Vaux would visit jewelry shops. He would ask to see rings, brooches and other small items. Then while he looked the shopkeeper in the eye, he would slip one or two items into his coat-sleeves, which he had had made specially wide. This gave him an income of about £10 a week. During the evening he would go to the theatre; there, dressed like a fashionable gentleman, he mingled with the crowds. He enjoyed the company, he enjoyed the plays, and he made a handsome profit for himself by picking pockets.

At home he made himself as good a reputation as he could. He paid his rent regularly, he paid all his bills and he completed this picture of a respectable gentleman by marrying an attractive young lady.

This lady was more than a good wife to him. She was a valuable accomplice. She would attract the attention of a shopkeeper, while her husband robbed the counter; she would flirt with a gentleman in the theatre while Vaux picked his pockets; she took the things that he stole, so that if he was suspected he would not have the goods on him. Between them, Vaux and his wife made a very good living for themselves.

But it was a dangerous life. Vaux had already served one sentence, and he only needed to be caught again and he would either be hanged, or transported for life. Sometimes things went wrong.

One evening at Drury Lane theatre Vaux came under suspicion. A gentleman said he had been robbed and accused Vaux. Several other people who had lost things remembered that Vaux had been standing near them, and there was a general clamour that he should be taken to the police. Vaux put on his most lordly air, and some of the accusers began to waver. Then one of Vaux's friends came up and told the others how wrong they were to blame someone who was obviously a gentleman and warned them of the danger of making false accusations. After a good deal of grumbling the crowd finally dispersed. During this time Vaux's wife had been watching helplessly. The shock was too much for her, and she was seriously ill for a long time.

Another time Vaux was busy in the theatre when he saw a gentleman using a valuable silver snuff box. Vaux sidled up to him, slit his pocket with a pair of scissors, and made off with the snuff box. He had no one with him, so it was a problem to hide the box for the time being. Accordingly he went to a public house near the theatre and gave the box to the landlady. He asked her to fill it, and said he would call back for it when the play was over. This, he thought, was a clever idea, but when he returned for the box he had a shock. As he took it from the landlady, he felt a hand on his shoulder and turned round to face the owner of the box and with him a Bow Street Runner.

Unfortunately for Vaux, the stable boy at the inn was a sensible lad. Quite by chance he overheard the owner of the box grumbling about his loss, and knowing that his mother had a snuff box in the bar, he took the man in to inspect it.

Vaux protested his innocence, but they searched him and found the pair of scissors. Now it seemed that nothing could save him.

Vaux spared no expense to hire the best lawyer he could for his defence. He dressed himself expensively, but plainly, put on a modest air, and went into the dock carrying a snuff box, so as to create the impression that he usually took snuff. He had also given a false name and luckily for him his previous conviction did not come to light. His story was that on the night of the theft he had left his own snuff box at home. The stolen one he had found, and had decided to borrow it for the evening. He had, he said, no intention at all of keeping it.

He stuck to his tale: he remained calm and confident; he spoke and looked like a perfect gentleman. The prosecution, moreover, were unlucky in their witnesses. They were no match for Vaux's clever lawyer, and soon began to contradict themselves. The jury found Vaux not guilty.

Vaux had now reached a point where he scorned all danger. Perhaps he knew that sooner or later he must be caught and he began to be careless.

One day he strolled into the shop of a jeweller called Bilger. He sat down and demanded to see some diamond rings. A lady came into the shop and while the shopkeeper turned to her, Vaux swept three of the rings into his sleeve. He then claimed that everything in the shop was too cheap for him, but promised to return to order an expensive ring that he would have specially made. Mr Bilger bowed him out, and Vaux, as he went, helped himself to a gold clasp and a brooch that he gave to his wife as presents.

He then decided on a very rash act. He thought that if he returned to the shop, he would remove all suspicion from himself, and that the lady who had come in after him would be blamed. Accordingly he went into the shop a few days later, and, not surprisingly, had rather a cool reception. Mr Bilger pretended he had nothing to show him, but offered to take his order for a diamond ring. His assistant came forward with a notebook. Vaux gave his instructions, and then went away congratulating himself on his cleverness and good fortune. Surely, he thought, Mr Bilger would not suspect him now! He was wrong. The shop assistant had not written an order for a ring, but instead a description of Vaux that was accurate to the smallest detail.

A few days later Vaux had a shock. He had pawned one of the rings, as he had decided he would like to keep it for himself. When he went to redeem it the pawnbroker's assistant asked him to wait while he went to see his master. Vaux knew what that meant. The shop-assistant had gone, not for his master, but for a police officer. Vaux turned and fled.

He knew now that the police had circulated a description of the stolen rings and he knew, too, that there would also be some kind of description of himself. Had he known how accurate this description was, he would have been horrified.

Vaux and his wife moved to new lodgings, and for a month he did not stir outside. Mrs Vaux sold or pawned their belongings one by one, but when they were all gone, Vaux realised he would have to go out to 'work' again.

He arranged to meet an accomplice one evening at a public house. He knew that the Bow Street Runners frequented this inn, so it was a bad place to choose. He was also foolish enough to go out in the very clothes he had worn to Mr Bilger's shop. On arriving at the inn, Vaux sent his wife to see if there were any police officers there, or if any were expected. The coast was clear, so he went inside. Mrs Vaux begged him to be as quick as he could, but Vaux had been too long cooped up in his house to wish to return. He insisted on remaining, and he stayed too long. Glancing up, he saw two Runners come through the door. He pushed his hat over his eyes and turned his back, but it was too late. A voice behind him said, 'Mr Vaux, we want you!'

Once more Vaux prepared thoroughly for his trial. He changed his clothes, he shaved off his whiskers, and he put on his most gentlemanly behaviour. It was all no use. Mr Bilger, his assistant and the pawnbroker all identified Vaux quite positively, and nothing could shake them. The jury found him guilty, and the judge sentenced him to death.

As was not unusual, the death sentence was changed to transportation for life, but this was bad enough. Wives sometimes went with their husbands, but Mrs Vaux was not given permission. Vaux begged that he should be allowed to sail at once. This, too, was refused. He spent a year in the filth and misery of the hulks before he left for Australia.

When finally he went he was only twenty-six years old. But he never returned to England, and he never saw his wife again.

3   The Police before Peel

Before 1829 the police system in this country had grown like an untidy plant.

In London the City had its own force, as it still does, and for those days it was quite efficient. Outside the City, in the remainder of London, it was a different story. Each parish made its own arrangements. Thus we find:

1. Parochial constables, unsalaried.
2. Watchmen, appointed to serve the constables.

In addition there were three types of police not organised by the parishes:

1. Bow Street officers and patrols.
2. A few salaried police officers attached to police offices.
3. Salaried water police, for duties on the Thames.

Key people were the Justices of the Peace. Then as now they tried most of the cases brought to court, and they also had important police duties which they have since lost.

We will now look at each of these officials in turn, to see how they had developed.

JUSTICES OF THE PEACE

Justices of the Peace date back to the Middle Ages; it is difficult to say exactly when they began, but they became particularly important during the Tudor period. They were unpaid, and often did not have offices or court rooms. Usually they conducted their business from their own houses. On p. 22 you can see a county magistrate in his own house, trying a poacher.

Unfortunately, in the early eighteenth century, magistrates earned a rather bad reputation. Too many of them were 'trading justices'. These men looked on their work as an opportunity to make money, and some of them accepted bribes

Before the Magistrate

totalling up to £1,000 a year. On p. 23 you can see a cartoon by Hogarth of a group of magistrates.

Eighteenth-century justices were concerned with police matters in ways that modern magistrates are not. They appointed the constables and were responsible for supervising their work. When a criminal was arrested they would question him before his trial as a C.I.D. officer does today.

On p. 23

CONSTABLES

We first hear of the constable in 1252, in the reign of Henry III. From the seventeenth century onwards we find him working closely with the Justice of the Peace. His duty was to bring offenders before the Justice. Another important duty was to organise the watchmen and see that they did their duty.

The constable wore no uniform and he earned no salary. Everyone had to take his turn to be constable and most men

Magistrates—a cartoon by Hogarth

found the duties an unwelcome burden. A constable served only for a year, and at the end of his time, gave up thankfully. Rich men would not do the work themselves. When it was their turn they paid someone to take their place. The result was that their duties were often performed by ignorant and unsuitable men.

WATCHMEN

As the medieval towns began to grow, the authorities found that the system of unpaid constables was not good enough. Because of this they appointed men to keep watch. Cities created or increased their force of watchmen as they found it necessary. London's force, for example, was considerably increased in the reign of Charles II. From that time onwards London watchmen were known as 'Charleys'. The watchmen, unlike constables, worked full-time and were paid.

There is no reason why a force of watchmen should not be

efficient. That in the City of London was. It was said that you could always recognise a pickpocket in the City because he walked quickly and often glanced over his shoulder. In greater London, however, and indeed in most of the rest of England, the watch was inefficient. Someone wrote this mock-advertisement:

'Wanted, men for London Watchmen. None need apply for this lucrative situation without being the age of 60, 70, 80 or 90 years; blind with one eye, and seeing very little with the other; crippled with one or both legs; deaf as a post; with an asthmatical cough that tears them in pieces; whose speed will keep pace with a snail, and the strength of whose arm would not be able to arrest an old washer-woman of fourscore returning from a hard day's fag at the wash-tub.'

The watchmen were laughed at and sometimes assaulted. Their attackers were often criminals, but sometimes they were men who should have known better. Young men in search of

Milling a Charley or Two

excitement would go 'Milling a charley or two'. On p. 24 you see two watchmen being assaulted. There were noblemen who, for some reason, took a strong dislike to watchmen. One of them had his servants hold a watchman to the ground, while his coachman drove over him.

BOW STREET RUNNERS AND PATROLS

Bow Street is a famous name in the history of the police force. It goes back to the early eighteenth century when a Justice of the Peace named De Veil set up his office there. It was, however, the two men who followed De Veil who brought real fame to Bow Street.

The first of these was Henry Fielding who became a Justice of the Peace in 1748 and remained in office until he died in 1754. The second was Henry's blind half-brother, John Fielding, who became a Justice in 1750 and did not retire until 1779. It is unusual for a blind man to be a magistrate, but like many blind people, John Fielding's other senses were unusually acute. He could recognise as many people by remembering their voices as a normal person can be remembering their faces.

Henry Fielding

John Fielding

On p. 25 you can see a picture of these two men. It was Henry Fielding who had the ideas, but his work was ably carried on by John.

Among his other gifts, Henry Fielding was a writer. He wrote books to make people realise the evil doings of criminals. These included 'An enquiry into the Causes of the late Increase in Robbers' and a novel, 'Jonathan Wild the Great'.

Fielding did his most important work in 1753, when he set up a force of full-time paid constables, later known as the Bow Street Runners. In the next chapter you can read about one of the last of the Runners, Henry Goddard. Bow Street Runners were detectives. Being detectives, they wore no uniform, but they carried a short staff with a crown on the end, as a symbol of their authority. It was easy to conceal, but they could show it when it suited their purpose. For example Henry Goddard once waved his at a coachman who was about to drive away, and the man stopped. When he was protecting a visiting nobleman, the Grand Duke Alexander of Russia, he showed his staff to the crowd. The crowd fell back at once. The Grand Duke was astonished and asked to see the little staff.

Runners drew a salary of a guinea a week, but this was little more than a *retaining fee*. They also had a share in the rewards for captured criminals. They could expect three or four pounds out of a £40 reward. Two fortunate runners were employed as court detectives, and this earned them £200 a year. Sometimes they watched for pickpockets in the theatres, and for this they were paid a guinea a night. Most of their money, however, they earned in their work as private detectives. Anyone who could afford the cost could hire a runner. The runner would charge a fee of a guinea a day, with an extra fourteen shillings for expenses. If he was successful, he would expect a reward.

Some people have accused the Runners of spending too

much time in the company of rogues. Criminals met together in taverns and gambling dens called 'flash houses'. One of these was in Bow Street itself! Runners visited the flash houses regularly, and this helped to earn them a bad name. But it is difficult to see what else they could have done. A detective is no better than his information allows him to be, and modern detectives do much as their Bow Street predecessors did. They mix with villains of all kinds in order to learn what they can. Frequently one criminal will inform on another out of jealousy, to pay off an old score, or, in the days of the Runners, for a reward. Probably the worst that can be said of the Runners is that they would overlook the doings of a petty thief, if he gave them information about an important criminal.

In 1763 there was another venture from Bow Street—John Fielding started horse patrols. At about the same time—we do not know exactly when—he started foot patrols. Their main duty was to put down footpads and highwaymen. The foot patrol survived but as the horse patrol was expensive, John had to withdraw it. It was revived, however, in 1805. This was the first Police force in England to have a proper uniform. The mounted patrolman wore a black leather hat, a blue greatcoat, blue trousers, white gloves, Wellington boots, and the scarlet waistcoat that gave him the nickname 'Robin Redbreast'. He carried a *sabre*, pistol, truncheon, and handcuffs. As he rode his beat in the dark he greeted travellers with the reassuring call, 'Bow Street Patrol!'

The new patrols did excellent work. For example, Hounslow Heath, which had been notorious for highwaymen, now became safe to travel across at night.

POLICE OFFICES

On p. 28 you can see John Fielding in his Court at Bow Street. This Magistrate's Office was such a success that after a lot of argument the government decided that there should be others

John Fielding in his Court at Bow Street

on the same lines.

In 1792 Parliament passed the Middlesex Justices Act. This set up seven Public Offices, which were known popularly as Police Offices, and later as Police Courts. Each had three salaried magistrates, earning £400 a year. In addition to the magistrates each office had six paid police officers whose work was very similar to that of the Bow Street Runners.

An important result of this Act was that the old 'trading justices' went out of business. The new offices did good work, but it was unfortunate that they did not work more closely both with each other and with Bow Street. A curious incident shows how little they worked together. In 1814 someone discovered that three members of the Bow Street Patrol were earning double pay by serving also on the staff of the Worship Street Police Office.

THE MARINE POLICE

As a result of the efforts of a magistrate called Colquhoun the

West India Merchants set up a river police force in 1798. Two years later, Parliament intervened and set up a new Police Office, with the usual three magistrates who were to be responsible for the river and its shipping.

You can see that by 1800 there were in all nine Police Offices. The first was Bow Street; next came the seven set up by the Middlesex Justices Act; finally there was the Marine Police Office. There was later to be a tenth, more famous than all the rest. It was set up in 1829 and, although its official address was 4 Whitehall Place, it had a doorway into Scotland Yard.

PRIVATE EFFORTS

As the police system was so inadequate it is not surprising that private people made their own arrangements to protect their lives and property.

The government itself encouraged ordinary citizens to help by offering rewards. You could earn anything from £5 to £40 depending on the importance of the criminal you caught. These rewards were known as 'blood money'. In 1815 a total of £80,000 was paid out in this way.

This system offered too many opportunities to men with quick wits and no scruples. These were the professional 'thief takers'. The most notorious was Jonathan Wild. Here you can see a picture of Wild.

Wild pretended to be an honest citizen, anxious only to recover stolen property and bring thieves to justice. He created for himself the imaginary office of 'Thief-taker

Jonathan Wild

29

General' and carried a little staff as an emblem. He was, in fact, the king of the London underworld. It was true that he did hand criminals over to justice, but these were men who had challenged his authority, or men for whom he had no further use. Wild used the threat of the hangman to keep discipline in his gang. It is true, too, that Wild recovered stolen property, but quite often it had been taken in a robbery he had planned. People who had lost things came to him to say what was missing. They would soon have a message from Wild to say that he had the goods, and would be pleased to return them—but that the finder must, of course, be rewarded. Wild's business grew to such an extent that he had warehouses for the storage of goods, and opened offices where people could come to make their enquiries.

Wild's career ended suddenly in 1725. He had made too

Jonathan Wild in the Condemned Cell

many enemies among both thieves and honest men. He was convicted of robbery and hanged. On p. 30 you see a picture of him in the condemned cell.

No one ever equalled Wild, but men like him continued to thrive in a smaller way for another hundred years or so. This was bound to happen as long as the government and private citizens continued to offer rewards big enough for men to make a good and easy living working for them.

PARLIAMENT AND PUBLIC OPINION

With so much crime and disorder you may find it surprising that Parliament did so little to put matters right. M.P.s knew the remedy—an efficient police force. They were continually being told what to do by people like Colquhoun who wanted a police force. It would be unfair to say that Parliament was indifferent. Indeed, before Peel passed his famous Act in 1829 there had been no less than seven Committees of Inquiry, the first being in 1770 and the last in 1828. But Committee after Committee turned down the idea of a proper police force.

The problem was that English people knew about the police of France and other continental countries. There they were more like a secret police, and the police officer would act as a government spy. Englishmen felt that theirs was one of the few free nations in the world, and believed that if the government had a well-organised police force at its disposal, that freedom would be in danger.

The only action Parliament was able to take you have already seen. This was to increase the number of Police Offices from one to nine. It was a useful reform, but was not nearly enough to cope with the criminals of that period.

4   Henry Goddard—Bow Street Runner

Henry Goddard, Bow Street Runner

Goddard was born in 1800. The picture shows him in his old age, but it is not difficult to imagine how he looked when he was young.

When he was twenty-four he joined the Bow Street Foot Patrol. He was soon promoted for in 1826 he became a runner for the Great Marlborough Street Police Office. This meant he was now a detective. In 1834 he joined the Bow Street Runners and remained with them until they disbanded in 1839.

In 1840 he became the first Chief Constable of Northamptonshire and held this position until 1849 when he had to retire because of an injury. He had always done private detective work and after 1849 this became his chief interest.

Goddard was a remarkable man. His courage was amazing, and he several times arrested men in the face of mobs anxious to protect them. He kept cool and used his judgment wisely in all sorts of conditions—although he does admit that he trembled with excitement as he broke open a trunk and found it contained £1,000 of stolen money. He said, 'The perspiration poured down my face and made me feel so excited that I felt as though I was committing a robbery and expecting detection every moment.'

Certainly Goddard had his faults. He was vain, snobbish and extravagant. He was a little too fond of good food and good wine—often his accounts tell us more about the food he ate than how he caught his criminal. As against this he had many qualities. Once he had caught his man, he treated him with kindness and consideration. Above all, he was a brilliant detective. He was highly intelligent, he had great imagination and he seemed to know by instinct what line of enquiry he ought to follow and how the criminal would try to escape. Nor would he give up until he had exhausted every possibility. At sixty-five he traced a criminal all the way to Melbourne in Australia. Earlier he followed a man to New York where he lost all trace of him. Goddard went inland on what seemed an impossible task. Finally he found his man, as he put it, 'at a log hut, on a Prairie near the Rock River with his trousers tucked up, mowing wet grass in the territory of Wisconsin, U.S.A., 2,000 miles from New York'. It was a sad blow to discover that, under American law, he could not arrest him.

During this trip to America, someone tried to rob his bedroom. He suspected two men, but could prove nothing. Later on, in England, he heard that two Americans had been arrested for stealing. Goddard went to see if they were the men he had suspected in America. They were not—but then, they might have been, and Goddard was not the man to leave any stone unturned. It was this dogged persistence that brought him many successes.

Here are some of Goddard's cases.

MR SPRING'S WATCH
In 1824, when Goddard was still a humble patrol man, he was sent on duty to Drury Lane Theatre, along with a senior detective named Nettleton—a surly and unpleasant fellow. As the audience was going in a young lady came running to say her friend, Mr Spring, had been attacked by footpads who had made off with his watch. Mr Spring had called 'Stop Thief!' in a loud voice but no one had come to his aid and the

thieves had escaped through Covent Garden Market. Nettleton thought that the robbers would be far away and could not be caught. Goddard thought a little longer and suddenly vanished with a linkman. When he returned Nettleton reprimanded him for leaving his post and asked in a sarcastic way if he had the thief. 'No,' said Goddard, 'but I have the watch!'

He reasoned like this: Mr Spring had called 'Stop Thief!' in a loud voice. Therefore the robbers would have thought they were being chased. The only safe thing to do when you are being chased with a stolen watch in your possession is to throw it away. Goddard and the linkman had searched the market, and sure enough, there was the watch, lying among some cabbage leaves.

MADAME VESTRIS

This lady was an actress. One day she went to a rehearsal and left her coach outside the theatre in charge of her coachman and a page. She had a purse containing four £5 notes which she hid under the cushions. On her return both purse and page had vanished.

Goddard was called in and went to work methodically. Madame Vestris gave him a full description of the page and her bank gave him the numbers of the £5 notes. The coachman was able to tell Goddard quite a lot. He said the young man had often wanted to go to the West of England, but since he had no money to pay a coach fare he would travel, as the poor did in those days, by wagon.

Goddard now made enquiries at the inns from which the wagons departed, and found that one was due to leave the following day. He determined to be there when it left. It was a long shot, but it was worth a try. Accordingly he rose early in the morning and went to the inn yard. He was pleased and surprised to see a young man who answered the description Madame Vestris had given him; he was even more excited when he saw him change a £5 note. Going to the innkeeper, Goddard said who he was and asked to see the note. Sure enough it was one that had been stolen. Goddard at once arrested the lad and Madame Vestris recovered most of her lost money.

THE ARREST OF DICK POUCHER

This case did not involve any clever detective work, but is a good example of Goddard's courage.

In 1829 there had been a burglary in a house in Lincolnshire, near Stixwould. The local constable raised the Hue and Cry and two of the gang were soon caught and executed. Others, including Dick Poucher, escaped. An Association for the Prosecution of Felons offered a £100 reward for information leading to Poucher's arrest. In 1830 Poucher turned up in Warwickshire with a group of navvies digging the Oxford canal. One of his mates, Joe Bealey, recognised him and went to London where he contacted Goddard. Goddard set out for Warwickshire with another runner named Schofield. Joe had to go along as well so that he could point out Poucher when they arrived.

On arrival at Rugby, Goddard and Schofield went to see the local constable. He said he would really need twenty soldiers to take Poucher from the gang of navvies, but he volunteered none the less. He arranged for two enormous blacksmiths, the brothers Tring, to come along. These two men were sworn in as Special Constables, and off they went. Joe now had cold feet. He said he wanted his reward money, and would go no further. Schofield said that if he did not carry out his part of the bargain, he would tell the other navvies how he had informed on Poucher and leave him to his fate. This scared Joe so badly that he agreed to go on.

The party approached the inn where the navvies took their evening meal. They left a *post-chaise* near by, but out of sight, while Schofield sat on a stile and Goddard went into the inn with Joe. Joe pointed out a huge navvy he said was Poucher and at once fled to London to claim his reward. Goddard watched Poucher finish his supper, and leave the inn with several other navvies all carrying pickaxes and shovels. As long as they walked towards the post-chaise, Goddard followed, but when they turned aside, there came the moment he was dreading. He went to Poucher and told him he was under arrest. Poucher raised his shovel and would have felled Goddard, had not Schofield come behind him with a pistol and threatened to shoot. The Rugby constable and the Tring brothers now came up. Poucher flung himself on the road, dragging his attackers with him, and shouting to his mates to rescue him. Goddard had the presence of mind to give a boy on a pony half-a-crown to gallop off for the post-chaise, and after more struggling, Poucher was handcuffed. By now the other navvies had recovered from their surprise and a large number advanced along a hedgerow with their pickaxes and shovels. While the rest of their party dragged Poucher into the chaise, Schofield and Goddard stood at a gap in the hedge and held the navvies at bay with their pistols. Then they jumped on the roof and the terrified driver started the chaise with such a jerk that the two runners nearly fell into the road. The navvies rushed forward and pelted the fugitives with flints, but the horses soon outstripped the pursuers, and the adventure was over.

Goddard and Schofield were not the men to illtreat even a prisoner like Poucher. When he calmed down they replaced his evil smelling clothes, they let him take a warm bath and they fed him well. He looked and felt a new man. He begged them to say nothing of the fight, otherwise, he said, he would surely be hanged.

A few days later the two runners arrived at Lincoln with their prisoner, and over the castle gate the wretched Poucher saw the heads of his partners in crime. Goddard does not say whether or not he reported Poucher's behaviour at the time of his arrest, but probably he did not. The court did not order Poucher to be hanged, but sentenced him instead to transportation for life.

JOSEPH RANDALL

This is a case in which you can try your own skill.

Randall was butler to a Mrs Maxwell. One night he claimed he heard someone trying to burgle the house and his mistress afterwards allowed him to keep a pistol. Some weeks later the house was broken open, the silver cupboard was forced and its contents packed into hampers. The burglars had decamped, leaving the silver. This was Randall's statement.

'I saw a bull's eye lantern held at arm's length, with the shadow of a man before it, and a man behind the one that carried the lantern.

'They shone the lantern in my face and I pretended to be asleep. When they left, I waited a minute and then reached for my pistol under the pillow. At that moment a shot was fired through a hole in the shutter hitting the pillow where my head had been.'

Randall claimed he then jumped from his bed and struggled with the burglars who escaped, but left the stolen goods.

Something in this statement caused Goddard to suspect the butler. Can you see what it was? You will see the answer on p.100. You will also see how Goddard finally proved his suspicions were correct.

PART TWO

THE REFORM OF THE POLICE

5 The New Police

In Chapter 3 you read how unwilling people were to have a proper police force because they feared it would interfere with their freedom. A few, like Sir Robert Peel, saw that this idea was wrong. As he said to the Duke of Wellington: 'I want to teach people that liberty does not consist in having your house robbed by organised gangs of thieves and in leaving the principal streets of London in the nightly possession of drunken women and *vagabonds*.'

Wellington agreed. In 1828 he became Prime Minister and chose Peel as Home Secretary. Peel decided that his chance

Sir Robert Peel

had come. That same year there was the last of the many Parliamentary Committees set up to examine the need for a new police force in London. This one reported in favour of the idea. Peel went ahead and prepared his Metropolitan Police Bill, which became law in 1829.

You will remember that a large number of different authorities had been responsible for law and order in London. A main reason for the lack of organisation was that no one had overall charge. Peel said, 'I consider the whole of the district as one great city.' Consequently his Act swept away the police powers of all the separate parishes and gave them to the Home Secretary. The Home Secretary was to set up a new Police Office and appoint two Commissioners of Police to organise a force of some 3,000 men. The boundary of this area ran from four to seven miles from Charing Cross. Here there were to be no more parish constables of the old kind, no more watchmen and no more Bow Street Foot Patrol. The cartoon below shows Peel doing away with the watchman.

PEELING A CHARLEY

The Act did not make a clean sweep. This was more than Peel dared attempt. The most important exception was the City of London. Though it is right in the heart of the Metropolitan area the City remained responsible for its own police, as it still is. In 1829 there remained also the following:

1. The Bow Street Horse Patrols.
2. The officers attached to the existing Police Offices. These included, of course, the river police and the Bow Street Runners.

In spite of these exceptions Peel's Act was a big step forward. It was now possible to have an efficient police force in the Metropolitan area.

Passing the Act of Parliament was only the beginning. All the work of raising the new force and organising it still had to be done. This was to be the task of the two new Commissioners of Police.

The first two Commissioners were Colonel Sir Charles Rowan and Richard Mayne. Here you see pictures of these men.

Colonel Sir Charles Rowan

Richard Mayne

Rowan had had a distinguished career in the Army. He had served under Sir John Moore and the Duke of Wellington. He had fought through the long, gruelling *Peninsular War* and at

Waterloo. When he became Commissioner of Police he was forty-seven years old. Thanks to his military life Rowan was used to commanding large numbers of men. He was also good at organisation, and was a fine disciplinarian.

His colleague, Richard Mayne, was quite different. He was a lawyer by training and in 1829 was working as a *barrister*. He was only thirty-three, and, like most young barristers he found it difficult to make a steady income. This was a grave handicap, as he wanted to be married. Consequently, when he was offered the post of Commissioner of Police at £800 a year he accepted at once. Unlike Rowan, Mayne had not been used to commanding men, but he could still be very useful. His training meant that he could deal with the many legal problems the police had to face, and he was also good at drawing up regulations.

The two Commissioners had equal authority, so it was important that they should work together. Fortunately they became friends almost at once and remained so until Rowan retired in 1850.

As you already know, the Commissioners set up their office at 4 Whitehall Place—a house that had a back entrance to Scotland Yard.

One of the first things that Rowan and Mayne had to do was to recruit the new police constables and organise them into their various groups. They divided the Metropolitan area into seventeen divisions. In each division there was to be a Company. In every Company there were 144 constables, organised into sixteen sections, each nine strong. In charge of each section there was a sergeant, and in charge of four sections there was an inspector. The whole company was commanded by a superintendent. Within a year over 3,300 men had joined the force and all seventeen divisions were fully manned.

While they were gathering their recruits, Rowan and Mayne

were deciding how their policemen were to work. They set out their ideas in a book of Instructions for their constables: 'It should be understood at the outset that the principal object to be attained is the Prevention of Crime.' This still remains the main object of police work. Of course, once a crime has taken place, the police must try to catch the offender, but it is far more valuable to prevent the crime in the first place.

What kind of men joined the new force? Rowan and Mayne did all they could to find the best. Even police constables were carefully examined. Each candidate had to be able to read and write—many people could not do so in those days. He also had to produce testimonials to prove he was of good character.

Men from all walks of life joined the force, but not surprisingly, many of them were ex-soldiers. Those chosen to be officers were nearly all of them former *N.C.O.s*. Most of the Superintendents had been sergeant-majors in the Guards or the Cavalry. Naturally Rowan favoured soldiers, as he was used to handling them and they, in turn, were trained to accept discipline and danger.

Here you can see a group of 'Peelers' and on p. 43 you can

Peelers

Police Inspector on Duty

see an inspector talking to two suspicious characters. The inspector has a horse as he has to cover a lot of ground.

In spite of all their care, Rowan and Mayne were due for a shock. The first parade was on 29 September 1829. Unfortunately it was a rainy day, and many of the constables did not like being wet. When the rain began to fall numbers of the men in the ranks opened their umbrellas. You can imagine the effect this had on Colonel Rowan and the serjeant-majors who were present. Worse was to follow, for when they inspected the men, the Commissioners found that several of them were drunk. Ill-luck dogged the new police for some time. Of the first 2,800 to be enlisted, over 2,200 were eventually dismissed or resigned.

There were several reasons for this. The pay was not good and attracted men of good quality only if they were unemployed. As soon as they could go back to their old trades clerks and *artisans* left the force immediately. However, as on the first day, the chief problem was drink. The official reports said sadly:

'The Commissioners have again to express their regret that the pay day has not passed without some cases of intoxication, which compels them to dismiss the individuals who have been guilty of that crime.'

POLICE AND PUBLIC

As there had been so much opposition to the idea of a police force, it is not surprising that when the new police appeared in the streets for the first time, many people turned against them. Naturally, criminals hated them, but even honest citizens jeered at them and insulted them. Poor, ignorant people could perhaps be excused, but men who should have known better were also hostile. When the police tried to regulate traffic, noblemen bitterly resented it, and ordered their coachmen to use their whips, or even run over policemen. Newspapers complained about them. If there was crime or disorder, they accused the police of neglecting their duty; if the police made some arrests, then the papers said they were brutally assaulting the innocent public. Most serious of all was the attitude of the magistrates. Before 1829, as you know, the magistrates had had charge of all the constables and watchmen. Now these were gone, and in their place were the new police, over whom the magistrates had no control at all. Many of the magistrates showed their jealousy by obstructing the police in every way they could. In fact, they took sides with the public against them.

A police serjeant called Lacy one day found a man striking a woman. Lacy arrested him. To take revenge the man charged Lacy with assault. The court sentenced the unfortunate serjeant to two months' imprisonment and he even had to remain in prison after this time as he could not pay the expenses of his trial. Another time a mob attacked a group of policemen. They nearly killed one, seriously injured three and hurt a further eight. The magistrates did not even punish the ringleaders; they just bound them over to keep the peace. One day a particularly evil mob picked up a policeman and flung him onto some spiked railings. The punishment for the leader was only a £1 fine. The worst incident took place in 1833. A small group of police put down a serious riot. Several of them were badly injured and one, Constable Culley, was stabbed to death. The court found that the killing was *'justifiable homicide'*. This time they went too far. A Select Committee of the House of Commons looked into the whole affair and decided that the police had been blameless. Many members of the public felt sorry for Constable Culley's widow, and there was a subscription for her. People were beginning to realise, too, that the police were doing their best to put down crime and violence, and were not trying to destroy the liberty of honest citizens. Gradually suspicion and hatred of the force died down, though it has never quite vanished.

SUCCESS OF THE NEW POLICE

How far were the new police successful in their fight against crime? One writer says that within the first three years after 1829 the value of goods taken each year in thefts, burglaries, and robberies fell from £990,000 to £20,000. This seems too good to be true and we can hardly believe in such startling success. Certainly the number of ordinary crimes dropped, though by how much we cannot tell. There was, however, one type of crime over which the police scored clear success. This was in dealing with riots.

In the early 1830s there was a good deal of discontent

among the poor. Unscrupulous men took advantage of this discontent to stir mobs to violence, hoping even to lead them to revolution. As a result there were riots. At first the only action the police took in face of a riot was to line the streets and defend themselves when attacked. Later they took to dispersing small groups before a mob could assemble, but this depended on having accurate information, and having it in good time. The solution came from a most unlikely source. One of the *radical* leaders of those times was Francis Place. Place saw that violence was doing his cause more harm than good, so he decided that the mobs must be put down. Accordingly he suggested to Superintendent Thomas of F Division that he should try a *baton* charge. The next time a mob gathered the rioters had the surprise of their lives. A group of determined police faced them, and instead of waiting to be attacked, they charged, waving their batons. The mob scattered and fled.

6   The Growth of the Metropolitan Police

The rapid growth of London and the changing pattern of crime meant that there had to be changes in the Metropolitan Police. But before we look at these changes, we had better learn something about the men in charge—the Police Commissioners.

We have already seen how Rowan and Mayne took charge in 1829, and we know that they worked well together. This partnership lasted until 1850, when Rowan retired. A Captain Hay took his place, but unfortunately he and Mayne disagreed. The quarrel between the two Commissioners caused a scandal.

But Captain Hay was not to remain a Commissioner for long. He died in 1852. The Home Secretary decided that it would be better to have one Commissioner only, and this has been the rule ever since. Consequently Mayne commanded the Metropolitan Police on his own until he died in 1868—a period of thirty-nine years. So powerful was he, that people called him 'King' Mayne. As he grew older he began to lose his grip; he made mistakes, and the force did not develop as it should have done. However, in spite of the mistakes of later years, Mayne will always keep his place in history, as one of the founders of our first modern police force.

Colonel Edmund Henderson succeeded Mayne. On p. 48 is a picture of him. Apart from his military experience he had been for twenty years governor of a convict settlement in Australia. Henderson was popular with the men. He allowed them to wear beards and change into ordinary clothes when they came off duty. Outsiders were worried that under an ex-colonel the police force might become too much like an army. Bruce, the Home Secretary, replied that he would have no objection to appointing a civilian, but where could he find

47

Colonel Edmund Henderson

one who had been used to commanding a force of 10,000 men?

Under these men and their successors, the Metropolitan Police increased their authority and the area they controlled. They also grew in numbers and their duties multiplied.

If you look back to p. 40 you will see that in 1829 the police Commissioners did not control all the police in their area. Henry Goddard, for example, worked without consulting the police at all.

This ended in 1839, when Parliament passed the Metropolitan Police Act. Magistrates now lost all their police duties. This meant an end to the police officers attached to the old police offices, including, of course, the Bow Street Runners. It meant, too, that the Thames Police became part of the Metropolitan Force, as did the Bow Street Horse Patrol.

Moreover, in 1839 the Metropolitan Police considerably

increased their area. They became responsible for everything within about fifteen miles of Charing Cross, which was approximately the ground that the Bow Street Horse Patrol had covered.

THE FIGHT AGAINST CRIME

As you already know there are fashions in crime, and the problems which the police have to face change as time goes on.

You saw in Chapter 5 that the police learnt how to stop riots. None the less, riots still broke out on occasion. It is not possible to describe them all, but this is what happened at three of them.

In 1840 someone told the police that 800 men known as Chartists were going to meet and plan a revolution. Police to the number of 350 approached the meeting place. While 250 stayed in reserve, the others burst in and arrested all the conspirators who were carrying arms. This sudden action gave the conspirators such a shock that they gave up all idea of organised violence. (You can read about the Chartists in another book in this series.)

Trouble of another kind came in 1855. Lord Robert Grosvenor introduced his Sunday Trading Bill. This ordered that shops and public houses should close on Sundays. Many of the working people were most upset. In those days men worked for six days a week. Only on Sunday could they relax and really enjoy a pint of beer or have the luxury of a shave at the barber's. Lord Robert's Bill would mean an end to all that. Someone wrote:

> 'Sublime Decree, by which our souls to save,
> No Sunday tankards foam, no barbers shave,
> And chins unmown and throats unslaked display,
> His Lordship's reverence for the Sabbath Day.'

Some people showed their disapproval by rioting. The police dispersed them but not before many of the rioters had been injured. There were the usual complaints of police brutality, and a Royal Commission looked into the matter. One witness described a certain Inspector Hughes: 'He was on a pale horse, and pale did he look, and *diabolical* was his countenance.'

There were further riots in 1868, this time in connection with the Reform Bill. Out of 600 police who were there, 265 were wounded. Again the rioters were dispersed, but this time the public were more sympathetic.

You can see from this cartoon that by now 'Punch' too, was on the side of the police.

RUFFIANLY POLICEMAN
ABOUT TO PERPETRATE A BRUTAL AND DASTARDLY ASSAULT ON THE PEOPLE.

Most of the riots that took place in the nineteenth century were political. People rioted either because Parliament made a law they did not want, or refused to make one they did want.

There were other crimes that were political and they were the work of the Irish.

They began in 1867 with a gunpowder explosion in Clerkenwell. The prison there housed two Irish rebels. Their companions tried to engineer their escape by exploding a barrel of gunpowder against one of the walls. Four innocent people were killed, and forty were injured—and all the time the rebel prisoners were in another part of the building.

Later the conspirators grew more ambitious and started using dynamite. This was in the 1880s. Here you see a picture

The attempt to blow up Government Offices in Charles Street, Westminster

of one of the Irish outrages.

Of course there was plenty of other crime. Particularly

alarming was an outbreak of *garrotting*. This took place in the 1860s. A garrotter first selected his victim, then crept up behind him and grabbed him suddenly round the neck with

Garrotting

both arms. When he had choked him, he robbed him. To protect themselves some people wore spiked collars.

No account of crime in the nineteenth century would be complete without some mention of the man nicknamed 'Jack the Ripper'. His real name we shall never know. This unknown murderer struck in 1888. In nine months there were eight murders, four of them certainly Jack's work and possibly five. So horribly did this man *mutilate* his victims that superstitious people feared that Cain or Satan had visited the earth.

Fortunately the killings stopped as suddenly as they had begun. The murderer was never caught.

Ordinary crime is not spectacular; it is small, mean and unpleasant. It was this more than riots and sensational murders that occupied the police for the greatest part of their time. This table shows how successful they were. It gives the number of people sent to prison for each 100,000 of the population:

Committals per 100,000 of Population

1841	175
1851	156
1861	91
1871	72
1881	57
1891	40

Are the police having similar successes at the present day?

THE IDENTIFICATION OF CRIMINALS

This is a vital part of the fight against crime. Once a criminal has been arrested, it is very important to find out who he really is. For one thing a hardened villain can give false names each time he is caught and pass himself off indefinitely as a first offender. The important work of identification is the duty of the Criminal Records Office, which began work in 1869 when Scotland Yard started a register of habitual criminals. This was some help, but often it was still difficult to prove that a criminal was the person whose name was already on the register.

Then a man called Sir Francis Galton came forward with an idea—why not use fingerprints? In certain eastern countries it had been known for some time that no two people have the same fingerprints. A man who could not write, would put a thumbprint on a document, instead of a signature. But Scotland Yard could not use Galton's idea at once. When a man is arrested it is easy to take his fingerprints—but on the files there are many thousands. It would take days of work to compare the new set with all those already in stock! The answer came from India. Sir Edward Henry, Inspector General of Police in Bengal, discovered a way to *classify* fingerprints. Scotland Yard adopted his system in 1901. Within the first twelve months they identified correctly four times as many criminals as they had ever done in any previous year.

The Metropolitan Police came into being in 1829, but there were no detectives at Scotland Yard until 1842. There were two main reasons for this.

In the first place Rowan and Mayne believed so strongly that the duty of the police was to prevent crime, that they were unwilling to admit the need for detectives. Secondly the public distrusted detectives even more than they did the uniformed police. A detective really did seem like one of the continental secret police. So strong was this idea that policemen had to remain in uniform even when they were off duty. Of course there were times when a policeman might have to put on civilian dress as a disguise. In those days they called it wearing 'coloured clothes'! Unfortunately one over zealous coloured clothes man did much to increase the prejudice against detective work. He was Constable Popay.

In 1833 Popay disguised himself as a working man and joined a body calling itself the 'National Political Union of the Working Classes'. Popay suspected that this organisation was planning a revolution, and he was determined to find out. All might have been well had he been content to sit quietly at the meetings and observe; Popay, however, took an active part and encouraged the other members in their daring schemes. It all came to an end when one of the Union members looked

54

through the window of a police station and saw Popay sitting inside, obviously very much at home there!

There was such an uproar that Popay was dismissed from the force and a Select Committee of the House of Commons looked into the whole question of using coloured clothes. They decided that policemen in disguise should only detect crimes and prevent breaches of the peace. To stir people up and encourage them to commit an offence so that you could then arrest them was 'most abhorrent to the feeling of the people and most alien to the spirit of the constitution'.

So strong was the prejudice against detectives that when the Bow Street Runners and the other officers were disbanded in 1839 there was no attempt to replace them. Admittedly a man might be taken off the beat for a short time to do detective work, but this is no substitute for a regular detective force. Before long, however, a famous case showed the weakness of this system.

One day a coachman called Daniel Good visited a tailor's shop. After he had gone the shopkeeper thought he had lost a pair of trousers. The shopkeeper was wrong—Good had not taken anything. However, a Constable Gardener set off after the missing trousers. He began to search the stable at Wandsworth where Good worked, and as he was poking about in the hay, saw something suspicious. At this Good leapt for the door, slammed it and barred it from the outside. Of course P.C. Gardener should have broken the door and run after his man. Instead he turned to examine the hay. He did not find any trousers—the thing in the hay was the dismembered body of a woman. By the time poor Gardener had recovered from the shock, and had smashed his way out of the stable, Good was clear away. All that Gardener did then was to send for his Superintendent, who arrived two hours later. Even then there was no pursuit. Instead the Superintendent ordered a thorough examination of the stables. Only then did he have

Good's description circulated. By the time this was published, Good had had twelve hours in which to make his escape.

Following the circulation of the description, reports came in from all over the place, and the police were quite confused. One Inspector, however, was lucky. He traced a cabdriver who had given Good a ride. This driver even remembered the address that Good had wanted. The Inspector should have watched the house carefully and in secret, but instead he went up to the front door and asked the woman who answered, whether Good was inside. Of course, the woman denied all knowledge of him. 'Never mind,' said the Inspector. 'Here is a leaflet describing him. If you see him, perhaps you will let me know.' The woman was Good's wife and only the day before she had helped him pawn his old clothes to buy new ones. Quite likely her husband was hiding in the house while the Inspector was innocently believing her every word at the front door! However that might be, Good had a timely warning, and once again made his escape.

Daniel Good, however, was a most unlucky man. The chase only began because he had been wrongly suspected of stealing. It ended because of an even more remarkable coincidence. Good made his way to Tonbridge. How was he to know that in the town there was a workman who had once been a policeman in 'V' Division at Wandsworth—the place where he had once been a coachman? The ex-constable recognised him and reported him at once. This time Good was arrested. The final success of the police was, however, not due to their skill or efficiency. They were very lucky to have a third opportunity to make the arrest, having bungled the first two. The public recognised this and Rowan and Mayne set up a proper detective force.

The Detective Branch came into being in 1842. Its offices were in Scotland Yard, and for the first time the London police began to use this famous name. The new force was not strong

—only two inspectors and six sergeants. For Rowan and Mayne prevention of crime was still the most important duty of the police. Over twenty-five years later, when Mayne retired, there were only fifteen detectives in the entire Metropolitan Police Force.

After this things began to move. In 1867 there was the explosion at Clerkenwell. Then in 1868 old 'King' Mayne retired and Sir Edmund Henderson became Commissioner. He increased the detective branch from fifteen to 200 and later on to 260. The new detectives were to discover the criminals of their own areas, to keep them under observation and learn all they could from them. This was one way in which the Bow Street Runners had worked, and it is still in use today.

In 1878 the Detective Branch had become so important that it was completely reorganised. It became the Criminal Investigation Department, with its own Assistant Commissioner in charge.

Here is an account of some of these early detectives and their cases.

THE MURDER OF CARLO FERRARI
You probably know that in the early part of the nineteenth century hospitals would pay money for dead bodies. The students *dissected* them in order to learn *anatomy*. One day four men arrived at King's College hospital with the body of a boy, later identified as an Italian, Carlo Ferrari. The demonstrator of anatomy was suspicious. The body was obviously healthy, and there was no obvious cause of death. There was, however, a small cut on the side of the head which could have been the result of a struggle. The demonstrator kept the men waiting, as they thought for their money. In fact he sent for the police, and the four men were arrested. As yet, however, there was no case for them to answer, as there was no sign at all of the cause of death.

Superintendent Thomas took charge. He made a thorough search of the house where the suspects lived and in a well he found a shawl that he traced to a Mrs Rigburn who had recently vanished without leaving any trace. Why, thought Superintendent Thomas, should her shawl be in the well and nothing else? Then he saw the answer. The murderers drowned their victim in the well, then let the body hang upside down, until all the water had drained from it. This would have left no cause of death obvious. It was while she was hanging upside down that the shawl had slipped from Mrs Rigburn's shoulders.

Superintendent Thomas now intensified his search. Policemen dug over the garden thoroughly and found other clothes buried there. There was now quite enough evidence to hang the murderers.

THE ARREST OF TOM PROVIS

Provis was an imposter. The police had all the evidence they needed to convict him, but they could not find out where he was. In charge of the hunt was Inspector Field.

Field's chance came when he heard that an old woman of the Provis family was living in Warminster. But, even assuming the old woman knew anything, how could he persuade her to betray her own relation?

Field went to Warminster and passed by the cottage where the old lady was living. On catching sight of her he stopped and stared. 'My word,' he said, 'you remind me of my mother—you are exactly like her.' They then fell into conversation. Field said he had been unwell, and had come to the West of England for a holiday. He was, he said, looking for lodgings. The old lady found him so pleasant that she offered him a room in her own house.

For several days Field was the perfect lodger. The old lady was glad of his company, and they spent hours in friendly

conversation. When Field thought that he had won his landlady's confidence he decided to try his luck. He started to
complain about his bad relations. The old lady was full of
sympathy. 'Why,' she exclaimed, 'one of our family, Tom
Provis, is the greatest rascal living.' At last the conversation
was going the way Field wanted. To help progress he suddenly
complained of stomach ache and produced a bottle of gin,
which was, he said, the only cure he knew. It was only
natural, thought the old lady, that he should invite her to
share the bottle with him. Under the influence of the drink
she began to talk even more freely and in the end told Field
all that he needed to know in order to find and arrest Provis.

THE ROAD-HILL HOUSE MURDER

Road Hill House is in Wiltshire, near the Somerset border. In
1860 the Kent family lived there. They were unusual people.
The father was Samuel Kent—an overbearing man, hard on
his family and unpopular with his neighbours. His first wife
had died, having shown some signs of insanity. The youngest
child of this marriage was a girl called Constance. In 1860 she
was sixteen years old. She was a passionate, determined girl,
and had once shown her spirit by running away from home.

Mr Kent had married again. Neither he nor his new wife
cared anything for Constance, especially since there were more
children by the second marriage. The favourite was Francis, a
child of three. He had his own room, where he slept with his
nurse, Elizabeth Gough.

One day Francis vanished. There was consternation, and
everyone hunted for him. They found him at last, with his
throat cut and with stab wounds in his chest.

Mr Kent was very unpopular with the neighbours, so they
suspected him. However, Superintendent Foley of Trow-
bridge suspected the nurse, Elizabeth Gough, presumably
because she had the best opportunity. The Wiltshire police

could make no progress, so Detective Inspector Whicher arrived from London. Whicher had already made a name for himself as a detective. This was to be his most famous case—it was also to be his last.

Whicher examined the facts, and he suspected Constance. He noted the girl's high spirits and temperamental nature, and he saw, too, how she hated her stepmother. How better could Constance show her hatred than by killing the stepmother's favourite child?

Whicher had only one clue. Constance had lost a nightdress. She had an innocent enough explanation—it had been lost in the wash. But had it? Just before the laundry basket had been taken away, Constance had sent the maid on an errand which gave her the opportunity to take anything she wanted from the basket. Admittedly the maid had seen nothing strange about the linen—certainly none of it was bloodstained. But did even this clear Constance? She had three nightdresses in all. Whicher reasoned in this way. She murdered the little boy, and her nightdress was stained with blood. This was the one she hid until she could destroy it. Now she had to make it seem that it had been lost in the wash. She took her second nightdress from her drawer to wear and put her third one in the laundry basket. She kept it there for the maid to see until the last possible minute, then she sent the maid away, took out the nightdress from the basket and returned it to her drawer. The basket went almost at once to the laundry, and the alibi for the missing nightdress was complete.

It was not easy to prove all this. Whicher arrested Constance, hoping that the shock would make her confess, but she was stubborn. Whicher might even now have made progress, but everyone turned against him. The local magistrates released Constance, and Superintendent Foley even suppressed evidence. One of his men had found a bloodstained garment—almost certainly the nightdress. Foley had ordered him to put it back where he found it. When the police had gone to look for it again, it had vanished. But Foley kept these vital facts from Whicher, perhaps to hide his own incompetence.

In the face of all this, Whicher resigned. He had made himself heartily disliked. Like all of us the local people wanted to see an unpleasant person arrested for the murder, and in their view this was Samuel Kent. Instead Whicher had arrested a mere girl of sixteen.

Unfortunately Richard Mayne allowed himself to be too much influenced by the popular clamour, and he accepted Whicher's resignation.

The murder remained unsolved. Then, in 1864, for no apparent reason, Constance Kent confessed that she was guilty. She was sentenced to penal servitude for life, but was released after about twenty years.

However, there are still some doubts. Did Constance have some unselfish motive for shielding the real criminal? This idea inspired Yseult Bridges to write the novel 'Saint—with Red Hands?' You could read this, if the Road-Hill House murder interests you.

THE TRIAL OF THE DETECTIVES

This took place in 1877. It is a reminder that policemen, too, are human. They not only make mistakes, but can even go as far as crime themselves.

In the 1870s two men named Benson and Kurr perfected a system for swindling people who hoped to make large sums of money by betting on horses. For a clever swindler it is easy enough to persuade foolish people to part with their money. What is not so easy is to avoid arrest afterwards. Benson and Kurr thought they had found the answer. They met a detective called Meiklejohn and persuaded him to accept bribes. Later they learnt that Meiklejohn's superior, Chief Inspector Druscovitch was in debt. Druscovitch, too accepted a bribe.

Later another Chief Inspector named Palmer fell into the net. With three detectives on their side, Benson and Kurr felt safe. As soon as there was any danger of arrest, a timely warning would come from Scotland Yard itself.

All this had to end. It happened when Benson and Kurr became greedy and persuaded a wealthy French woman to place a bet of £30,000. To draw this money she had to see her lawyer, and he, of course, was horrified. He went at once to Scotland Yard and saw the man in charge, Superintendent Williamson. Williamson ordered the arrest of Benson and Kurr, and the three detectives who had accepted bribes were compelled to join in the hunt. As Druscovitch said to Kurr, 'I have got to arrest somebody'. Finally Benson and Kurr were brought to justice and received long prison sentences. Then came the moment the detectives feared. Hoping to have their sentences reduced, Benson and Kurr gave the names of the men they had bribed. Palmer, Druscovitch and Meiklejohn were convicted of conspiring to obstruct the course of justice and received the maximum sentence of two years' imprisonment.

Here now are some cases in which you can try your own skill as a detective.

THE ROBBERY OF MAJOR HAMPTON LEWIS

You have already met Superintendent Thomas who solved the murder of Carlo Ferrari. One day he answered a call from a hotel where a Major Hampton Lewis was staying. The Major had woken up in the night and found someone in his room. He had followed the man into the corridor where he had struggled with him. The robber escaped taking the Major's gold watch and purse. The only clue was a fragment of cloth torn from the thief's shirt, and another torn from his braces. Major Lewis was positive he could remember nothing of the man, but insisted that the police should search all London for his missing property. The Superintendent was more doubtful. 'How did you come to tear his shirt and braces?' he asked. 'Why, because he was without a coat,' replied the Major. 'Then you did know something of importance,' said the Superintendent. 'I hardly think we need to search far.'

What conclusion had the Superintendent reached?

CONSTABLE GOFF AND THE SHIRTS

One day a policeman named Goff saw a boy carrying a bundle of shirts. The boy was a well-known thief, so Goff stopped him. The boy was indignant. 'I have been to collect them for my father,' he said. Goff was about to let him go, when he had a sudden idea and felt the shirts. They were damp. At once he arrested the boy for stealing the shirts.

Why did he do this?

THE MURDER OF LORD WILLIAM RUSSELL

This murder caused a sensation, as Lord William Russell was an important man. Inspector Pearce and several other detectives investigated the crime.

The murder had taken place at Lord William's home. There were three servants in the house—a Swiss valet called Courvoisier, a cook and a maid. However, they knew nothing. The old man's body was in bed, where he had been killed during the night. Silver plate, jewellery and money were missing. Obviously the thief had disturbed the old man and killed him to prevent him from giving the alarm. The back door had been forced; the front door was open, apparently left that way by the burglar as he fled. There was also a bundle that he must have dropped in his haste. There was nothing much in it —just a few small things like the cook's silver thimble and a gold toothpick. It was this bundle that set Inspector Pearce thinking. What conclusion would you have drawn from it?

The answers to these problems are on p. 100.

PART THREE

THE REFORM OF THE PRISONS

7 From John Howard to Henry Mayhew

In this chapter and the next you are going to see how the prisons changed between the time John Howard was visiting them and the 1860s. Henry Mayhew, whose name appears in the heading to this chapter, lived in the middle part of the nineteenth century. He did much to show the wretched conditions poor people had to suffer, and he also spent much time and energy investigating prisons. In 1862, along with his friend Binny, he published his findings in a book called 'The Criminal Prisons of London'.

In chapter 10 you will see how the Government assumed more and more responsibility for prisons until finally it took them over completely.

ACTS OF PARLIAMENT

It was not long before Howard's work began to attract attention, and in 1773 he gave evidence before a Parliamentary Committee. He made four suggestions:
1. Sound, roomy, sanitary buildings.
2. Salaries for gaolers.
3. Training for prisoners, to help them reform.
4. Inspection of prisons.

At that time Parliament did not do much that Howard wanted, but a member called Popham brought in two Bills which became law. The first of these ordered that prisons should be kept clean, that prisoners should be washed, and that every prison should have its own doctor. The second stated that any prisoner found innocent should be set free in the open court, and not dragged back to gaol until he should pay his fees.

Then in 1823 came an important new law—Peel's Prison Act. This included all the four main ideas put forward by Howard in 1773, and more besides. Gaolers were not allowed to make money by selling food, drink and privileges. Female prisoners were to have female warders; a chaplain and a doctor were to visit the prisoners regularly; if a gaoler wished to use irons or chains, then he had to tell the local Justice of the Peace. Prisoners who were uneducated were to have instruction in reading, writing and religion.

All of these were excellent reforms, but Peel's Act, and indeed the ones that had gone before it, had a serious weakness. There was no way of making sure that the law was obeyed. The best that can be said of Peel's Act is that magistrates who genuinely wanted prison reform now had nearly all the powers they needed.

Ten years later, in the 1830s, Parliament took another important step. A Committee of the House of Lords met and reported on the state of the prisons. They were alarmed that there was much difference between prisons—some well ordered, and some still a disgrace; some too severe, and some lax. A man guilty of stealing would, in one prison, be living in filth and worked almost to death, while another, imprisoned for the same offence, could be living in comfort, with three good meals a day. The Committee advised that the Home Secretary should have powers of control. This was done by an Act of Parliament in 1835. The Home Secretary was to appoint Prison Inspectors and make grants for the upkeep of prisons.

Even so reform was slow enough. Prison reform meant an increase in the rates; the Government, however, was anxious not to force up the rates as this would make it unpopular. Consequently the prison inspectors were instructed to be moderate in their demands.

You can see, therefore, that Parliament had done the bare minimum. More than sixty years after Howard had given his evidence, Parliament had only tackled the worst abuses. Thirty years later, Henry Mayhew still found considerable differences between one type of prison and another, and so it was bound to be, as long as local magistrates had control, in spite of government inspection.

PRISON REFORM FROM 1774 TO THE 1820s

In view of the slow way in which Parliament was moving, it was fortunate that there were people who were willing to carry on Howard's work.

One of these was Sir George Onesiphorous Paul, a Gloucester magistrate. Later there was James Neild, Sheriff of Buckinghamshire. He, like Howard, wrote a book called 'The State of the Prisons'. But the most famous of all was Elizabeth Fry.

This remarkable woman was a Quaker. She was strongly religious, like Howard, but unlike him she was not afraid of the limelight. Calm, confident, and very sure of herself, she was responsible for a public crusade.

She made her first visit to Newgate gaol in 1813. With her went a friend called Anna Buxton, and both ladies carried with them bundles of clothing to give to the prisoners. The ladies were wearing their trim, neat Quaker clothes and Elizabeth had a watch pinned to the front of her dress.

They asked the gaoler to let them into the women's ward. He was horrified. The female prisoners, he said, were wild. There were thieves and murderers among them who would stop at nothing. Certainly it would be suicide to go in wearing a watch. The women would kill their visitors in order to steal it. Elizabeth quietly insisted that she and Anna should go in exactly as they were. Reluctantly the gaoler agreed. The turnkey opened the heavy gate; the two ladies stepped into the ward and the horde of filthy prisoners closed round them.

Exactly what happened then we shall never know, but Elizabeth Fry began to speak and gradually the noise and disorder died away. She and Anna gave out the clothing they had brought and after they had comforted the unhappy prisoners as much as they could, they left. Their clothing was still as neat as when they went in, and the watch was still pinned, undisturbed, on Elizabeth's dress.

Family cares prevented Elizabeth from visiting Newgate again for another four years, but she could not forget what she had seen there. As soon as she possibly could, she set about a thorough reform of the women's part of the gaol. She decided that these women needed education, discipline, useful work, and, above all, religion. Whereas Howard would have struggled on alone, she formed the Association for the Improvement of Female Prisoners in Newgate. This was a group of ladies willing to follow her example and visit the prison to do all they could to help.

Of course, they could not compel good behaviour—they had no authority—so they encouraged the prisoners to draw up a code of rules for themselves. This they did, and each woman promised to obey it. They started a school. Sometimes a lady visitor would give them a lesson, but more often the teacher would be one of the prisoners. The women formed working companies and made articles of clothing. The visitors provided the materials and sold the finished goods. Above all, the visitors did all they could to convert the women to the Christian faith, by reading the Bible, by talking to them, and by the example of their own lives.

In a short while this evil prison was transformed. In the women's ward at least there was no more filth, disorder and wickedness.

Elizabeth Fry was not content just to reform Newgate. Like Howard she travelled the country; but unlike Howard, she attracted all the publicity she could. There were meetings and discussions, while everywhere Ladies Prison Associations sprang up. These carried on Elizabeth Fry's work in her absence. The members visited their local prisons regularly; they did what they could to help the inmates; they made public all the evils that they found.

After the work done by Howard, all right-thinking people agreed that prisons should be clean and healthy. Many local authorities took steps to see that this was so. The main problem was now what to do with the prisoners.

It so happened that at this time the Americans were experimenting with two different systems. One was the Silent System and the other was the Separate System. Eventually both found their way to this country.

Under the Silent System, prisoners were together most of the time, but were never allowed to speak to one another. Under the Separate System, prisoners spent most of their time on their own, in individual cells.

There was a good deal of argument about which was the better method.

One man who believed in the Separate System was the Rev. John Clay, Chaplain of Preston Gaol.

Clay said that the results of the separate *confinement* were remarkable. Hardened criminals had once spent their prison sentence, joking, bellowing and brawling with their evil companions in the yards. After long weeks on their own, however, they softened and gave way.

This period of softening took several months of separate confinement. During this time Mr Clay would learn all he could about the prisoner, would come and talk to him, and would win his confidence by acts of kindness. Finally, when the solitude had done its work, the prisoner would break down, and would be willing to listen to the Chaplain's advice and accept his religious training.

The Rev John Clay

'As a general rule, a few months in the separate cell render a prisoner strangely *impressible*. The chaplain can then make the brawny navvy cry like a child; he can work on his feeling in almost any way he pleases; he can, so to speak, photograph his own thoughts, wishes and opinions on his patient's mind, and fill his mouth with his own phrases and language.'

Of course, everything depended on the personality of the chaplain. Not all the Chaplains were John Clays and prisoners found them easy to deceive. Warders told stories of convicts who learnt to recognise the sound of the chaplain's walk, and would fall on their knees as he approached. When the cell door opened, the chaplain would be delighted to 'surprise' the inmate at his prayers.

At Reading the chaplain's belief in religion went too far altogether. The prisoners were allowed very little activity. Clay scornfully remarks: 'The burglarious navvy was indulged in a little occasional knitting.' The prisoners spent the remainder of their time reading and learning by heart the Old and New Testaments. Convicts called the prison read-read-Reading Gaol.

There were, however, serious difficulties. Prisons working the Separate System had a high death rate. There were too many suicides, too much insanity. Even those who did not go

Solitary Confinement

mad suffered from terrible depression that damaged them physically and mentally. You can see from this picture how the artist Cruikshank pictured the effects of lonely imprisonment.

As early as 1799 the poet Coleridge wrote:

'As he passed by the Cold-bath Fields he saw,
A solitary cell:
And the devil was pleased, for it gave him a hint,
For improving his prisons in hell.'

THE SILENT SYSTEM

The theory behind the Silent System was quite different from that behind the Separate System.

There was no attempt to 'soften' the criminal by solitary confinement. Consequently there was no point in going to the expense of giving him a separate cell. All the warders did was to enforce silence so that the prisoners could not have a bad influence on each other. To prevent a man committing more crimes on his release, they relied, not on religion, but on fear. To this end they made prison life as unpleasant as they could. Today we believe in sending a man to prison AS punishment. Those who believed in the Silent System would have said that he was there FOR punishment.

Someone who believed this was Charles Dickens. Criminals fascinated Dickens, but his interest did not lead to any sympathy. 'It is a satisfaction to me to see the determined thief, swindler or *vagrant*, sweating profusely at the treadmill or the crank, and extremely galled to know that he is doing nothing all the time but undergoing punishment.'

There were several prisons willing to put these ideas into practice. They made prison life as unpleasant as possible, mainly by the two instruments mentioned by Dickens, the treadmill—more properly called the treadwheel—and the crank. There will be a fuller description of both later on. Briefly, working the treadwheel was like walking up stairs for long periods of time, and working the crank was like turning a mangle, or the starting handle of a car. Below you can see a prisoner at crank labour.

Crank Labour

At Leicester the authorities favoured the crank. Each prisoner was supposed to turn his machine 14,000 times a day. There was a scale of 'Fees' for meals—2,000 turns before you could have breakfast, another 5,000 before you could have dinner, and so on. At this time no tramps were to be seen within miles of Leicester—they were all scared of being put to crank labour in the prison.

Birmingham copied Leicester, and went even further. The deputy-governor, Austin, was a particularly brutal man. He demanded too much work from his prisoners, and cut their food when they did not obey. One lad refused to work the crank altogether and was punished so severely that he committed suicide.

Possibly hard prison conditions and labour amounting to torture may have deterred some from committing any more crimes, but we have no means of knowing how successful the treatment was.

So the argument went on. Was it better for a prison to deter: was it better for it to reform? There was no sure means of telling. One thing was certain. Anyone who went to gaol in those days certainly paid for his sins. Under one system, he stood a chance of being worked to death; under the other he could be driven insane by the long hours of solitude.

We will now look at two London prisons of Mayhew's time. One is Pentonville, which worked on the Separate System. The other is the Middlesex House of Correction, otherwise known as the Coldbath Fields Prison. This used the Silent System.

Pentonville belonged to the Government. Coldbath Fields prison was the responsibility of the Middlesex magistrates.

8 Prisons in the Eighteen-sixties

BUILDINGS. Below you can see a bird's eye view of Pentonville. The main part of the prison is built on 'the radial wing plan'. The cell blocks radiate from a central point, like the spokes in half a wheel. Thus anyone standing in the centre could command a view down all of the main corridors.

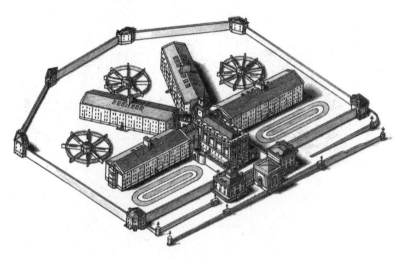

Pentonville Prison

Each of the four wings contained 130 cells. The next picture shows how they were arranged—in stories either side of the corridor. To reach the upper cells, you had to climb a flight of iron stairs and walk along iron landings. Connecting these landings at intervals were structures that looked rather like the bridge of a ship. In later years they found they had to stretch steel nets across. Convicts were in the habit of dropping things on people they disliked, or even jumping over the balustrade to commit suicide.

Prison Wing, Pentonville

Cells at Pentonville were nearly fourteen feet long, seven
feet wide and nine feet high. Each had its own wash basin, a

stool, a table, a hammock and a gas burner. Each cell even had its own W.C. Should a prisoner be taken ill then he could signal to a warder. He sounded a gong, and pulled down a metal plate, which stuck out from the outside of his wall at right angles.

The cells were roomy enough to take fairly big pieces of equipment. In this picture you can see the inside of a cell, with a loom. Of course, before he started work the prisoner would roll up his hammock.

Prison Cell, Pentonville

Heating was by hot air, blown up from below. They would not put in hot water pipes, as the prisoners would have used them for tapping messages to each other.

Ventilation was excellent. Air was drawn from the cells through ducts, and then into central ventilating shafts. You can see the ends of these shafts in the bird's-eye view. They look like large chimneys on the roof of each cell block. So light and airy was the building that Mayhew remarked: 'It strikes the mind as a bit of the Crystal Palace, stripped of all its contents.'

For water supplies, Pentonville had its own *artesian well*. The criminals here drank purer water than most of the honest citizens of London. Also the prison was perfectly clean. The same good order was everywhere.

In addition to the cell blocks, there were such places as a chapel, an infirmary, a kitchen and a house for the governor. Outside there were exercise yards. The two largest were on either side of the main entrance. Here the majority of the convicts exercised. For dangerous criminals there were individual yards. These were the wheel-like structures you can see in the bird's eye view. The prisoners walked around, each in his walled segment, while a warder watched from a platform in the centre of the circle.

To complete the security of the cells and the cell-blocks a high wall surrounded the prison.

Such a place would have astounded and delighted Howard.

Chief Warder, Pentonville

PRISON STAFF. By the 1860s most prisons had a proper staff of warders, under the control of a governor. The new warders and governors were far removed from the old turnkeys and gaolers of Howard's day. They were, of course, salaried, and there was no question of them extorting money from prisoners. Of the staff at Pentonville, Mayhew said: 'The governor is a kind-hearted gentleman, and the warders are a mixture between policemen and military officers.'

All of them could be firm with their prisoners, and many were excellent disciplinarians.

PRISON CLOTHES. The days when convicts wore grey clothes with broad arrows had not yet arrived. Each prison had its own uniform. At Pentonville the coat and trousers were a dull brown, but the most surprising thing was the cap. This had a large peak which would pull down over the face to form a mask. The convict was able to see through two slits. The object of the mask was to prevent the men from recognising each other.

PRISON FOOD. By the 1860s prisoners were no longer starving to death, as they had been in Howard's day. Instead people were wondering if they were not too well fed.

Henry Mayhew was impressed by the cocoa at Pentonville. In those days *adulterated food* was common in the shops, but in the prison they ground the berries with their own steam-engine, and used the water from their own artesian wells.

However, prison diet was hardly luxurious, as can be seen from this list of the Pentonville rations:

Breakfast. 10 oz. bread: ¾ pint of cocoa.
Dinner. ½ pint soup; 4 oz. meat; 5 oz. bread; 1 lb. potatoes.
Supper. 1 pint *gruel*; 5 oz. bread.

Since this prison was on the Separate System, prisoners ate alone in their cells.

WORK IN PRISON. As the aim of the Separate System was to reform criminals, most of the tasks at Pentonville were useful. There was work for the convicts as cleaners, cooks and gardeners. For the maintenance of the building there were a few carpenters, bricklayers and blacksmiths. Moreover, each cell was a workshop, where a man might learn or practice a trade. You have already seen a picture of a cell with a loom. In addition to weaving there was tailoring, shoe-making and mat-making. Twelve of the warders were qualified trade instructors, and during working hours they went from cell to cell, helping and instructing the prisoners and supplying them with materials.

EXERCISE. Prisoners needed exercise badly. Not only did it keep their bodies healthy, but it was good for their minds as well. When the authorities at Pentonville saw numbers of prisoners going insane they found that more exercise was part of the cure.

You can see the Pentonville convicts at exercise in the picture. Each has his mask down, so that he cannot recognise his friends, and they are holding a rope, knotted at five-yard intervals. This kept them at a fixed distance from each other, and so prevented conversation.

Convicts Exercising at Pentonville

PRISON DISCIPLINE. By the 1860s order in prison had to be no less than perfect. This was not easy. The worst were usually the boys and young men. Many of them had never known any sort of control in their lives and they found the discipline of the prison more than they could stand.

Once a prisoner in the *refractory cells* at Pentonville grew violent as he was being locked up. He all but bit off a warder's nose and the man backed out in a hurry. In the narrow corridor it was difficult to do anything. The prisoner would not mind about killing a warder, but the warder, of course, could not kill him. In the end they smoked him out with burning pepper.

Sometimes a prisoner who had shoe-making tools would become violent. This was particularly dangerous as he would have a hammer and a knife. The warders would wait for an opportunity, then fling open the cell door. One would bound forward with a large shield of basket work and others would come behind with weapons like huge pitchforks, bound with leather. They used these to pin the man against the wall. Later, they found that all this was not necessary. All they had to do was to cut the man's food to bread and water, and in a few days he would submit.

Punishments were of various kinds. At one time flogging had been common and though there were still tales of brutality, they were not usual. Most prison governors found it better to grant privileges for good behaviour, and then remove them if a prisoner gave trouble. There were also punishment cells for serious offenders. Here the prisoner's food was one pound of bread a day, with only water to drink. The cells were especially secure, with an iron grille inside the door. There was also as little furniture as possible. When the door was closed there was complete darkness. Henry Mayhew allowed himself to be shut in one of these cells at Pentonville for a few minutes, to see what it was like:

'The air seemed as *impervious to vision* as so much black marble, and the body seemed to be positively encompassed with blackness, as if it were buried alive, deep down in the earth itself.'

PRISON ROUTINE. This is Henry Mayhew's description of a day at Pentonville.

At 6 a.m. the prisoners woke up and started cleaning the prison. Each man was responsible for his own cell, and special groups cleaned the corridors. Cooks and bakers reported to the kitchen.

At 6.30 a.m. work began in the cells.

'The lower wards echoed with the rattling of looms, and we could hear the prolonged tapping of the shoemakers above, hammering away at the leather, so that now the building assumed the busy aspect of a large factory, giving forth the same half bewildering noise of work and machinery.'

Breakfast was at 7.30 a.m. The warders distributed the four hundred meals to the cells in ten minutes, placing the food on small ledges which fell down outside the windows of the cell doors.

At 8 a.m. there were morning prayers in the chapel.

'No sooner does the clock point to the hour, than the bell is heard booming throughout the *resonant* arcades, and instantly the cell doors are thrown open, and the brown clad prisoners stream forth from every part of the building; above, below, on this side, on that, lines of convicts come hurrying along the corridors and galleries at a rapid pace, one after the other, and each at the distance of some four or five yards, while the warders keep crying out to the men, "Now, step out there will you—step out".

'This is accompanied with a noise and clatter that is as bewildering as the sight—the tramping of the feet, the rattling of the iron staircase, the slamming of the cell doors, and the tolling of the bell—all keep up such an incessant commotion that the mind becomes half distracted with what it sees and hears.'

Below you can see a picture of the chapel. To stop conversation, each man had his own little cubicle and could see only the chaplain and some of the warders. The prisoners' heads, said Mayhew, appeared to be arranged in pigeon holes.

Chapel at Pentonville

The men enjoyed the service. Their responses to the chaplain were loud and enthusiastic, for this was one of the few times in the day that they could use their voices. They also liked the Bible stories.

After chapel they exercised until 9 a.m. when they returned to their cells and worked until dinner at 1 p.m. There then followed an afternoon of work until supper at 5.30 p.m. After supper the trade instructors went their rounds, issuing materials for the following day. At 7 p.m. work ended and the men could read in their cells for two hours. Lights out was at 9 p.m. The warders turned out the gas lights in the cells, dimmed the lights in the corridors, placed their cutlasses in readiness and put on felt overshoes. Everywhere there was silence and the only men active were the warders on night duty, keeping patrol to see all was secure.

THE MIDDLESEX HOUSE OF CORRECTION, COLDBATH FIELDS
BUILDING. This prison was much older than Pentonville (built 1794) and you can see from the picture opposite that it was not on the 'radial wing' plan. Instead there are different blocks, each for different types of prisoner.

As this was not the Separate System, there were buildings, such as workshops and dining rooms, where the prisoners met together. The original idea had been that each man should have his own cell for the night, but overcrowding meant that most of them slept in dormitories. Those who had cells were the unlucky ones. There was no heating, no lighting, poor ventilation and no means of attracting attention. Prisoners could have books, but did not have lights and so could not read throughout the winter months. The cells were so cold that it was not unknown for prisoners to die for lack of warmth.

FOOD. Under the Silent System the prisoners ate in a dining hall. This is a description of a meal at the Coldbath Fields Prison:

'Big tubs, filled with thick gruel, had been carried into the dining sheds, and a pint measure of the limpid paste had been poured into the tin mugs, and this, with a spoon and the 6⅔ ounces of bread were ranged down the narrow strips of tables that extend in three rows the whole length of the place.

'The men stood still for a second or two, until the order

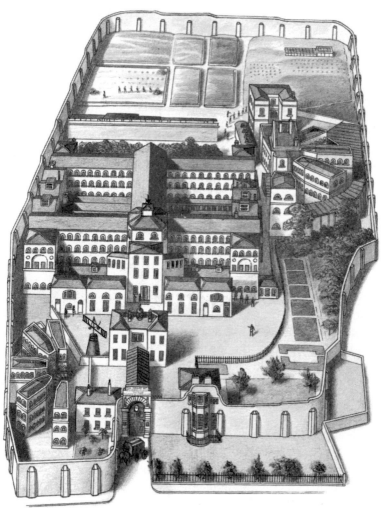

The Middlesex House of Correction, Coldbath Fields

was given to "Draw up table", and instantly the long light
dressers were, with a sudden rattle, pulled close to the men.
Then the warder, taking off his cap, cried "Pay attention
to grace!" and every head was bent down as one of the

prisoners repeated these words:

' "Sanctify, we beseech thee, O Lord, these good things to our use, and us to thy service, through the grace of Jesus Christ." A shout of "Amen" followed, and directly afterwards the tinkling of the spoons against the tin cans was heard, accompanied by the peculiar sound resembling "sniffing", that is made by persons eating half liquid messes with a spoon. Two prisoners, carrying boxes of salt, passed along in front of the tables, from man to man, while each in his turn dipped his spoon in and helped himself. The "good things", as the water gruel and bit of bread are ironically termed in the grace, were soon despatched and then the men, reaching each little sack of books which had been suspended above their heads, passed the remainder of their dinner hour reading.'

WORK IN PRISON. You will remember that the theory behind the Silent System, was that prison should be a deterrent. This meant that prison life had to be as unpleasant as possible, and to achieve this, the authorities relied mainly on work.

At the Coldbath Fields there were four kinds of work, all tedious and, all with one exception, completely useless. They were oakum picking, working the treadwheel, turning the crank and shot-drill. Oakum picking was the least objectionable in that it did produce something useful. It was, however, very monotonous. Henry Mayhew found this work going on in a huge shed. Five hundred convicts were in there, all working in a silence 'as intense and impressive as that of death itself'. They were so close together that it was impossible to see the forms on which they sat.

Should any prisoner raise his head from his work he would see on the wall the text: 'Go to the Ant, thou Sluggard, consider her ways and be wise.'

Oakum picking meant unravelling lengths of rope, and

picking all the fibres apart. Mayhew describes how they worked:

'Each picker has by his side his weighed quantity of old rope, cut into lengths about equal to that of a hoop-stick. Some of the pieces are white and sodden looking, whilst others are hard and black with the tar upon them. The prisoner takes up a length of junk and untwists it, and when he has separated it into so many corkscrew strands, he further unrolls them by sliding them backwards and forwards on his knee, until the meshes are loosened.

The strand is further unravelled by placing it in the bend of a hook fastened to the knees, and sawing it smartly to and fro, which soon removes the tar and grates the fibres apart. In this condition all that remains to be done is to loosen the hemp by pulling it out like cotton wool.'

Here is a picture of a prisoner doing this work.

Picking Oakum

The air was full of dust, and the prisoners who were new to the work had their hands covered with cuts and blisters.

In all the prisoners picked three and a half tons a week. The oakum was then sold so that it could be spun again and used for ropes or cheap mats. It fetched only £5 a ton, so that a week's work for five hundred men was not worth £20.

The men in the oakum room considered themselves lucky when they thought of those on the tread-wheel. The work there was completely useless. The wheel might have been used to work

85

machinery; instead it turned a huge fan. The prisoners described their work as 'grinding the wind'.

The wheel itself was a huge drum, sixteen feet in circumference. Around the outside were twenty-four steps, each eight inches apart. The prisoners called it 'an everlasting staircase'. The steps were rather like the floats on a paddle wheel. The prisoners stood with their backs to the warder, supported their hands on rails, and then moved their legs as if going upstairs. However, instead of going up, the stairs moved down under them. Apparently it was the want of a firm tread which made the exercise particularly tiring. The actual work, consisted not in turning the wheel, but in lifting the body each time the step fell away. There were twenty-four compartments along the length of the wheel, every other one being used at any given time, for the men worked fifteen minutes on and fifteen minutes off. You can see from the picture that every alternate prisoner is resting. The wheel revolved, twice a minute, and after every thirty revolutions a bell rang. The

Treadwheel and Exercise Yard, Coldbath Fields

men worked fifteen sessions a day, a total of four and three-quarter hours. During this time they 'climbed' the equivalent of 7,200 feet—more than twice the height of Snowdon.

The treadwheel fan stood outside the building. The length of its beam was twenty feet. Its purpose was to regulate the

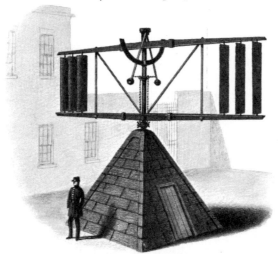

Treadwheel Fan

speed of the wheel.

Not surprisingly prisoners avoided work on the wheel if they could. They would drink too much water, take too much salt, eat soap, or swallow any rubbish that might make them sick. They would even injure themselves.

The crank machine was an iron drum, on legs, with a long handle, like a large starting handle for a car. Inside there was a circle of cups and a thick layer of sand. As the cups revolved they dipped into the sand at the bottom, and emptied themselves at the top. On the front of the machine was a dial plate which showed how many revolutions had been made. Working hard, it was possible to turn the handle twenty times a minute. A normal day's work was 10,000 revolutions, which would take about eight and a half hours.

Unlike Leicester and Birmingham in the earlier days, the crank was not in regular use at the Coldbath Fields. It was used as a punishment, or if a man complained about his work. A few days in solitary confinement, turning the crank, usually convinced him he was better off elsewhere.

For shot drill the men were lined up, three yards apart. At one end of the line was a pile of iron balls, each about the size of a cocoa-nut, and weighing 24 pounds. This is about the weight of a bucket, filled with water. Their work was to pass the iron balls along the line, until the whole pile had been shifted. They then passed them all back again. Moreover, they were not allowed to pass the shot from hand to hand. Mayhew describes the drill:

' "One!" shouted the officer on duty, and instantly all the men stooping, took up the heavy shot. "Two" was scarcely uttered when the entire column advanced sideways, three yards, until each man had taken the place where his neighbour stood before. On hearing "Three", they every one bent down and placed the iron ball on the earth, and at "Four" they shifted back, empty handed to their original stations.'

Shot drill was the hardest work of all. It could not go on for more than an hour and a quarter. But in that time the men had walked the equivalent of nearly two miles, sideways, picking up and putting down a twenty-four pound weight every three yards.

9 Transportation and Government Prisons

The transportation of criminals meant taking them overseas. Even in the Middle Ages, individual criminals were banished to foreign lands, but it was impossible to take them away in boat loads until the country had an overseas empire.

Transportation really began when the British settled in North America. It developed on a large scale when an Act of Parliament of 1717 allowed convicts to choose transportation instead of branding, whipping or sometimes even hanging. Quite a trade in convicts grew up. There were firms who specialised in it, like Messrs Stephenson and Randolf, felon dealers, of Bristol. They took the convicts, shipped them to the colonies and recovered their expenses by selling them. In 1740 a good, healthy felon would sell in the West Indies for about £80.

This trade came to a sudden end when the American War of Independence broke out in 1776. A few years later it revived, only now the convicts were going to Australia. Here the settlers were anxious to have all the cheap labour they could find, and at first they welcomed the convicts.

In 1787 Commodore Philips set sail with two frigates and seven transport ships holding between them 800 felons. They went to Botany Bay in New South Wales. In 1867 the last shipment went to the Swan River in Western Australia. In all during these eighty years, 150,000 criminals went from this country to Australia—at one time at the rate of well over 2,000 a year.

On arrival in Australia most of the convicts were assigned to settlers. In all justice a man's fate should have depended upon the seriousness of his crime, but assignment did not work that way. How a man fared depended partly on the trade he could offer and partly on the character of his master.

The least fortunate were the farm workers. They might well find themselves on a remote farm, many miles from civilisation and quite at the mercy of their masters. However, not all masters were bad and, in general, a convict farm worker in Australia was better off than a free farm worker in England.

Domestic workers were usually well-treated, and lived as members of the family, but the most fortunate were the skilled workers. As one settler explained: 'A convict who has been a blacksmith, carpenter, mason, *cooper*, wheelwright or gardener, is a most valuable servant, worth three or four ordinary convicts. He is eagerly sought after.'

A skilled worker would have money, rum and free time in which to enjoy himself. If he misbehaved in any way, more than likely his master would overlook it.

A number of convicts turned their transportation so much to their own advantage that they made their fortunes. One such man had only two good qualifications—quick wits and a dislike for rum. While he was under sentence he sold his rum ration to his fellow convicts so that when the time came for his release, he had enough money to buy a public house. Here he continued to do well. To farmers who wanted money he willingly made loans, and took the deeds of their land as security. When all their land was mortgaged, he demanded his money back. As they could not pay he took their farms. Within a few years he was one of the richest landowners in New South Wales.

Another man, a clerk, swindled a large sum of money from his employers. The police could not find the money, but the man was sent to Australia. His wife arrived there first, bringing the money with her. She then had her husband assigned to her as a servant, and the two settled down in their new homeland to live comfortably for the rest of their lives.

But for every convict who made his fortune, there were

many who suffered horribly. These were the men who were foolish enough to commit a further offence in Australia, while they were still serving their sentence for their crime in England. Some went to work in chain gangs. Under the heat of the sun they worked at stone-breaking and road-building, while at night they were crammed into wooden caravans to lie on the bare boards. Even these were lucky compared with those who went to the *penal settlements*. Someone said of the life in the penal settlements: 'Let a man be what he will when he comes here, he is soon as bad as the rest; a man's heart is taken from him, and there is given him the heart of a beast.'

One of these settlements was on Norfolk Island. The food here was bad and insufficient. When a man ate he had to pick up his food in his hands; knives and forks were not allowed.

For sleeping the men crowded into sheds. A visitor who saw the inmates coming out of one such hut was astounded that there were so many. When he went inside he saw the explanation. The men slept not only on the floor, but all round the walls on narrow shelves.

The work was hard and monotonous. Most of the men cultivated the land with no better implement that a large hoe. To make things worse, over half of them had to work in chains.

What made life really intolerable, however, was the discipline. The warders punished the most trifling offences by flogging, and these beatings were so severe that prisoners sometimes committed suicide to avoid them. One unfortunate habit was that of using favoured convicts as warders. These men were thoroughly unreliable. It sometimes happened that an unlucky prisoner would be reported and flogged for an offence he did not commit simply because a convict warder had taken a dislike to him.

After a mutiny in 1834 twenty-nine men on Norfolk Island were condemned to death. Later sixteen of them were reprieved and a clergyman went to tell them the news. The result was not at all what he expected:

> 'I said a few words to induce the men to resignation, and I then stated the names of those who were to die; and it is a remarkable fact, that as I mentioned the names of those men who were to die, they one after another dropped to their knees and thanked God that they were to be delivered from that horrible place, whilst the others remained standing *mute*.'

Transportation to Australia ended for two reasons. In the first place many people in England became uneasy. In 1838 a Parliamentary Committee of Enquiry reported on the evils of the system, and advised that it should end. Even more important, the Australians themselves began to resent their country being used as a human rubbish tip. Transportation to New South Wales stopped in 1840. In 1852 Tasmania refused to accept any more criminals and this meant that transportation virtually ended in that year, though a thin trickle went out to Western Australia until 1867. From then onwards Great Britain had to 'consume her own smoke'.

GOVERNMENT PRISONS

You will remember reading in chapter one that all prisons of the eighteenth century were the responsibility of the local authorities. But the law would often allow a felon to accept transportation instead of the death penalty. Should it prove impossible to transport him, then he remained the responsibility of the government. This problem was not serious until 1776, when the American War of Independence broke out, and, as we have seen, transportation stopped for the time being. The government took two measures. In the first place it decided it would have to build new prisons—but this would take time and cost a lot of money. Secondly it decided to take old warships and merchant ships, and convert them into floating prisons. This would be both quick and cheap. Old ships no longer fit to go to sea were known as hulks. The word 'hulk' took on a new meaning.

You will understand the difficulty of keeping a crowd of convicts clean, healthy, and in good order in an old ship gradually rotting away. At first the 'captains', as the gaolers were called, did not make any serious efforts. The result was that conditions were very bad. From August 1776 to March 1778, a period of about twenty months, more than a quarter of the prisoners died. The result was a public enquiry and the Government ordered some improvements.

However, in the early nineteenth century we still find complaints. A chaplain of one of the hulks said:

'In the close and stifling nights of summer the heat between decks is so oppressive as to make the stench intolerable, and to cause the miserable inmates frequently to strip off every vestige of clothing and gasp at the port-holes for a breath of air.'

There was a lack of supervision, so that there was much disorder. Fights were common and there were sometimes riots. The same chaplain said:

'The spectacle on board the Medway hulk when one prisoner was slain and twenty-four desperately wounded would have appalled any humane heart. The hulk was a perfect shambles, and a frightful scene of uproar, excitement and bloodshed. Suffice it to say that a mere handful of warders was powerless to deal with the armed mob below decks. All that could be done was to fasten down the hatches and when the work of butchery and *carnage* was over, descend below to fetch up the dead and wounded.'

As John Clay said, the hulks were:

'A place where goodness and reformation were almost as impossible to a man as his personal cleanliness would be were he to live in a common sewer.'

When Henry Mayhew visited the hulks at Woolwich in the
1860s he found conditions much better than they had been
earlier in the century. There was no dirt, no disease, and no
disorder. Here is a picture of one of the hulks.

The 'Warrior' Hulk

The 'Defence' hulk contained 500 convicts. There were
three decks, each one being divided into two long cages with a
passage between them. Here the convicts slept at night, in
hammocks so close together that they almost touched. Here,
too, they had their meals. In the daytime the hammocks were
rolled and put away, and tables which had been stacked for the
night, were pulled out and set. The convicts scrubbed the
tables every day and polished their plates and mugs until they
shone.

Food was much the same as in ordinary prisons—plain and
dull, but adequate. For breakfast there was bread and cocoa;
for dinner, meat, potatoes and bread; for supper gruel and

Ward set for Dinner, 'Warrior' Hulk

bread. Above is a picture of a ward set for dinner.

The whole ship followed strict routines. The convicts roused at 5.30 a.m., breakfast was at six, and by seven the first men left for work. So it went on through the day, everything punctual to the minute.

The convicts worked in Woolwich arsenal where they did all the heavy, unskilled work, cleaning the outsides of ships, piling timber, clearing rubbish, turning capstans, carrying coals, pulling carts, scraping shot, cleaning guns, and building fortifications. All were kept hard at work, since a warder would be fined one shilling each time one of his men was seen idle. On page 96 you can see convicts at work.

The most pathetic sight at Woolwich was the convicts' graveyard. It was a desolate field. Mayhew's guide drew his attention to a small, pale blue flower. It was called the 'convicts' flower' and, so the legend ran, grew only on the graves

Convicts Scraping Shot

of convicts. No stones or crosses gave the names of the dead;
instead the graves were marked only by low mounds which
soon vanished into the long, rank grass.

Convicts Building Fortifications

PERMANENT GOVERNMENT PRISONS

The use of hulks, and the revival of transportation, allowed the government to put off the day when they should need more permanent prisons. However, the first, Millbank, opened at last in 1821.

A second government prison opened in 1842. This was Pentonville, and you read about it in chapter 8.

The Government had to take further action in 1852, when transportation to Australia virtually came to an end. In the first place Parliament passed two Acts, one in 1853, and the other in 1857. Between them they substituted Penal Servitude for transportation. 'Penal' means 'punishment', and 'servitude' means 'hard work'. Under this system convicts spent the first part of their sentence under solitary confinement. They then went on to public works, as, for example, working in a royal dockyard, or arsenal. Finally, if their conduct had been good, they were released with a 'ticket-of-leave'. This meant they were virtually free, apart from a few minor restrictions, such as having to report to a police station from time to time.

Besides introducing the system of Penal Servitude, the Government had to provide more prisons. It was at this period that Dartmoor came into its own. It had been built for prisoners of war during the Napoleonic period, and had lain empty ever since. It reopened in 1850. It was first used for invalids from the hulks at Portsmouth, in the mistaken belief that the climate of the moor would be good for them.

THE PRISONS NATIONALISED

You have already seen how the Government became more and more interested in prisons. It set up prisons of its own—first the hulks, and later Millbank, Pentonville, Dartmoor and others. It also appointed inspectors to keep an eye on the prisons still under the control of local magistrates. The inspectors, however, ran into difficulties. Government grants covered only part of the cost of any improvements that became necessary; the local rates had to pay the rest. Most proposals for prison reform brought a lot of opposition from the rate-payers. There was only one solution—the Government would have to take complete control of all prisons. This happened when Parliament passed the Prisons Act of 1877. The prisons now became, as they still are today, the responsibility of the Home Secretary.

10   Conclusion

This story does not have a happy ending. Our police forces are, today, much more efficient than they were a hundred years ago, but they still solve less than half the crimes that take place. Modern prisons are as humane as their old buildings and overcrowded conditions allow. But in spite of this many men and women still go through prison and return at once to a life of crime. We still have our street hooligans, and we can easily imagine them joining in the Gordon Riots. We have thieves and pickpockets who would have made good companions for James Hardy Vaux. We no longer have horse thieves, but car thieves are just as bad. Our highwaymen do not hold up coaches, but we still have highwaymen who make off with lorry loads of valuable goods, and train robbers too.

What is the reason for all this crime? Two hundred years ago people like John Howard would have said that crime was due to poverty and ignorance. If only you could save everyone from starvation and give everyone a good education then, they thought, crime would almost vanish.

If we could bring John Howard back from the dead he would be amazed at the way we live today. Very few people go short of food. Almost everyone lives in a comfortable home with good food and clothing. Everyone goes to school until they are at least fifteen. Poverty and ignorance have almost vanished. Why then, is crime still with us? Howard would have been bewildered to see how much crime still goes on. No doubt his comments would be very interesting. What have you to say on this problem?

ANSWERS TO PROBLEMS

Page 37

If a man holds a lantern at arm's length, his shadow will be *behind* him, not in front!

Goddard went on to look at the jemmy marks on the doors and concluded that they were the work of an amateur. This, again, pointed to the butler. Proof, however, came from the bullet that had been fired. Goddard inspected the butler's pistol and his bullets. He saw that each one had a tiny pimple. He then inspected the mould in which the bullets had been cast and noted a little impression which explained the pimples. The bullet which went through the pillow had been flattened a little, but none the less it, too, showed the same tell-tale pimple. A gunsmith confirmed Goddard's opinion that the bullet was Randall's own. Randall was arrested and bit by bit his story came out. It was never his intention to steal the plate. He had invented the burglars, his close escape from death and his heroic struggle in order to win praise and a reward from his employer.

Fortunately for him, Mrs Maxwell decided not to prosecute and he was allowed to go free.

Pages 62-63

THE ROBBERY OF MAJOR HAMPTON LEWIS

Burglars do not roam the streets in their shirt-sleeves. It attracts attention! If the burglar had no coat he was almost certainly someone in the hotel. Superintendent Thomas searched the hotel and sure enough he found a man with a torn shirt, torn braces—and with the Major's wallet and watch under his mattress.

CONSTABLE GOFF AND THE SHIRTS

People do not deliver wet shirts. Wet shirts belong on clothes lines, and Constable Goff suspected the boy had been helping himself. It was not long before an angry housewife turned up at the station, asking if the police could help her recover her washing.

THE MURDER OF LORD WILLIAM RUSSELL

A thief who finds a few small things like a toothpick and a thimble does not waste valuable time doing them up in a bundle. He puts them in his pocket. Inspector Pearce suspected that the bundle had been dropped on the hall floor to give the impression of a man in flight—it would reinforce the idea given by the open front door. Possibly then the murderer was a member of the household. Pearce went on to discover that the marks on the back door not only fitted a bent poker in the house, but showed that the door had been forced from the inside. After a long and thorough search the police found the missing jewellery and plate hidden in the room of the valet, Courvoisier. This was enough evidence to have the man convicted and hanged.

THINGS TO DO

1. Imagine you have visited Newgate prison in the late eighteenth century. Write a report on your visit, saying what you found and saying what reforms were needed.

2. From your other history books, find out what you can about the Gordon Riots.

3. Why do you think it was a good idea to abolish public executions? Find out when this happened in England.

4. Give your opinions on the abolition of capital punishment.

5. Find an account of an eighteenth-century criminal, e.g. Dick Turpin, and describe his life in your own words.

6. Imagine you are Mrs Vaux. Write a story about your life with your husband.

7. Find a copy of Henry Fielding's 'Jonathan Wild the Great'. You may find it difficult to read, but you could attempt a chapter or two.

8. Imagine you are Dick Poucher. Describe your arrest by Henry Goddard, and say what happened afterwards.

9. Use your other history books to find out all you can about Robert Peel.

10. Put yourself in Peel's position. Write a speech intended to persuade Parliament to pass the Metropolitan Police Bill.

11. Organise a class debate on the topic: 'The prevention of crime is more important than its detection.'

12. With your Headteacher's permission, write to the Chief Constable of your area, asking him to send a member of the local force to speak to your class.

13. In what ways do ordinary members of the public (not criminals) show they dislike the police today?

14. Each member of the class should make two sets of fingerprints on pieces of card. Shuffle the cards together and then rearrange them in pairs. This will give you some idea of the difficulty of identifying finger prints.

15. Try to work out a scheme for classifying finger prints for yourself.

16. What difference would it have made to James Hardy Vaux if the police of his day had known how to use fingerprints?

17. Read parts of 'London Labour and the London Poor' by Henry Mayhew. You should also read 'London Life and the Great Exhibition of 1851' by J. R. C. Yglesias.

18. Read an account of the life of Elizabeth Fry, e.g. 'Elizabeth Fry' by Kathleen Bartlett.

19. Imagine you are a prisoner in solitary confinement. Write a letter to a friend describing your feelings.

20. Which prison do you think was more likely to turn a man from a life of crime, Pentonville, or the Middlesex House of Correction?

21. Find a book on modern prisons in your town library. What differences are there between a prison of today and one of Mayhew's time?

22. Look through some old newspapers in your town library and find out what crimes were committed in your area (*a*) fifty years ago (*b*) a hundred years ago. How do they compare with the crimes of today?

23. You can find out a great deal about crime and prisons in the nineteenth century from the novels of Charles Dickens. Ask your English teacher which of these books you should read.

24. Organise a class discussion on the topic, 'How to solve the problem of crime today'.

GLOSSARY

adulterated food, food sold with other substances added to it to make it seem more, e.g. plaster in flour

to alleviate, to relieve or help

anatomy, the study of the body

artesian well, well sunk deep into the chalk which lies underneath the clay of the London basin. The water from such a well is very pure. For a full explanation, look in your geography books.

artisan, a skilled workman, e.g. a cabinet maker

barrister, a lawyer: lawyers are of two kinds—barristers and solicitors; barristers do much of their work in court, cross-examining witnesses etc.

baton, a truncheon

carnage, killing

to classify, to put things into their classes, to arrange like with like. When things are classified it is much easier to find any individual item. The books in libraries are classified.

commitment, the act of sending someone to prison

cooper, a man who makes barrels

creditor, a person to whom money is owed

crow, a crowbar

confinement, imprisonment, the state of being locked up

diabolical, devilish, very evil

to dissect, to cut up a body in order to make a scientific study of it

effluvia, bad smells (singular; effluvium)

felon, a man convicted of a felony

felony, a serious crime, e.g. murder, burglary, robbery

garrotting, strangling someone from behind

gruel, a thin paste of oatmeal and water, like watery porridge

hulk, an old ship, not fit to go to sea, stripped of all her masts and fittings; hulks were sometimes used as prisons

impervious to vision, impossible to see through

impressible, easily impressed, easily persuaded or influenced

infirmary, a hospital

justifiable homicide, a killing which can be excused or justified, e.g. killing in self-defence

mute, silent

to mutilate, to damage, often by hacking with a knife or axe

nauseous, so unpleasant as to make one feel sick

N.C.O., non-commissioned officer, any soldier above the rank of private, but not an officer holding the Queen's Commission. Usually a corporal, sergeant or a sergeant-major

ordinary, a prison chaplain

Orpheus, a Greek who was supposed to have descended to hell

penal settlement, a settlement for convicts; a village where prisoners lived and worked.

Peninsular War, the campaign in the Spanish peninsula against the armies of Napoleon.

perjury, telling a lie after taking an oath to tell the truth

post-chaise, a light-weight coach, capable of being driven very fast.

proof, here means the first printing of a book: a proof reader will read this through to correct any mistakes before the book goes into production

radical, a politician who wants to carry out drastic reforms, rather than see things improve gradually

refractory cells, punishment cells

resonant, echoing

retaining fee, fee paid to a man even though he is not working: this fee gives one the right to call on his services at any time

sabre, a kind of sword

tap-room, a room where alcoholic drink is sold

transportation here means sending criminals overseas to serve their sentence instead of to prison

turnkey, old name for warder

turnpike, a toll gate

vagabond, see vagrant

vagrant, a wanderer, someone who has no home and no job. Vagrants often became criminals